AF227677

Australia
The Young Oldest Country

25 Ideas That Made Australia - Then and Now

Rahul Agrawal

For **Arjun** and **Navya** who asked the questions this country is still answering...

© Copyright 2026, All rights reserved.

TERRA NULLIUS
J. SMITH
AP AUSTRALIAN SONGLINES
SONGLINES - THE DREAMING
medicare
RAHUL AGRAWAL
For: 2020
COLOMAAANF
Donald Horne
The Lucky Country

Contents

Introduction

A Saturday morning in January, the middle of summer holidays. The family is at the kitchen table after breakfast. The back door is open and the heat is already coming in from the garden. Dad has spread a large map of Australia flat across the table, weighing the corners down with coffee mugs. Arjun is eating Vegemite toast and looking at the map. Navya is drawing her own version of Australia on a piece of paper beside it. Hers has a very large koala sitting in the middle of the continent.

Arjun: Australia is really big.

Dad: It is.

Arjun: But we live in a city. And most people live in cities. Why does it always feel like Australia is about the outback?

Dad: That is a very good question.

Navya: *(still drawing)* I am putting a koala in the middle.

Dad: There are not actually many koalas in the middle.

Navya: There are in mine.

Dad looks at the map for a moment.

Dad: This country is a strange and remarkable place. It is home to the oldest continuous human civilisation on Earth. And it is also one of the youngest nations. The same place, both things at once.

Arjun: How can it be both?

Dad: That is the question, isn't it?

Navya: *(looking up from her drawing)* Is the koala old or young?

Dad: Very old. Like most things in Australia that matter.

Australia is a young oldest country on Earth.

It is home to cultures that have endured for at least 65,000 years, the oldest continuous human civilisations anywhere in the world. And it is also a nation that is only 125 years old, one of the youngest federations on the planet. The same land holds both of these things simultaneously. That tension, between what was here before and what was built on top of it, between the ancient and the new, between the belonging and the arriving, is the central question of Australian life.

Most countries have a story they tell about themselves. Some stories are settled, agreed upon by most citizens and encoded in monuments and school curriculum and public holidays. Australia's story is not settled. It is argued about, revised, contested and slowly expanded to include voices that were previously left out. That argument is not a problem with Australia. It is, in many ways, the most honest thing about it.

This book follows a family living in Melbourne. Arjun is twelve, Navya is six and their parents are the same people who spent several evenings in the backyard wondering about the sky. Their neighbours Oliver and Mei appear from time to time. The conversations happen over summer holidays and long weekends, at barbecues and on road trips and in ordinary kitchens, as Australia unfolds around them. But Australia is a big country and these conversations travel further than just one city. They travel to Sydney and Darwin and Ballarat and along the Murray River and out to the vast red interior that most Australians have never visited but somehow feel they carry inside them.

The book is not a history of Australia, though it contains history. It is not a geography, though it contains geography. It is a book about the ideas that made this country what it is and what it might still become. Ideas about land and fairness and identity. Ideas about who belongs and who decides. Ideas about what a country owes the people it was built on and the people it invited in.

Some of these ideas are very old. Some arrived with European settlement. Some were forged in war or crisis or on a harbour shore on a January morning in 1788. Some are happening right now, in courtrooms and parliament and on Country and at kitchen tables exactly like the one where this family is sitting.

All of them matter. And all of them connect, in some way, to the land that Aboriginal Australians have known and cared for longer than any country on Earth has existed. That land is the oldest part of this story. It is also the part most of us are still learning to read.

It begins, as all good things do, with a child asking a question.

Timeline of Australia

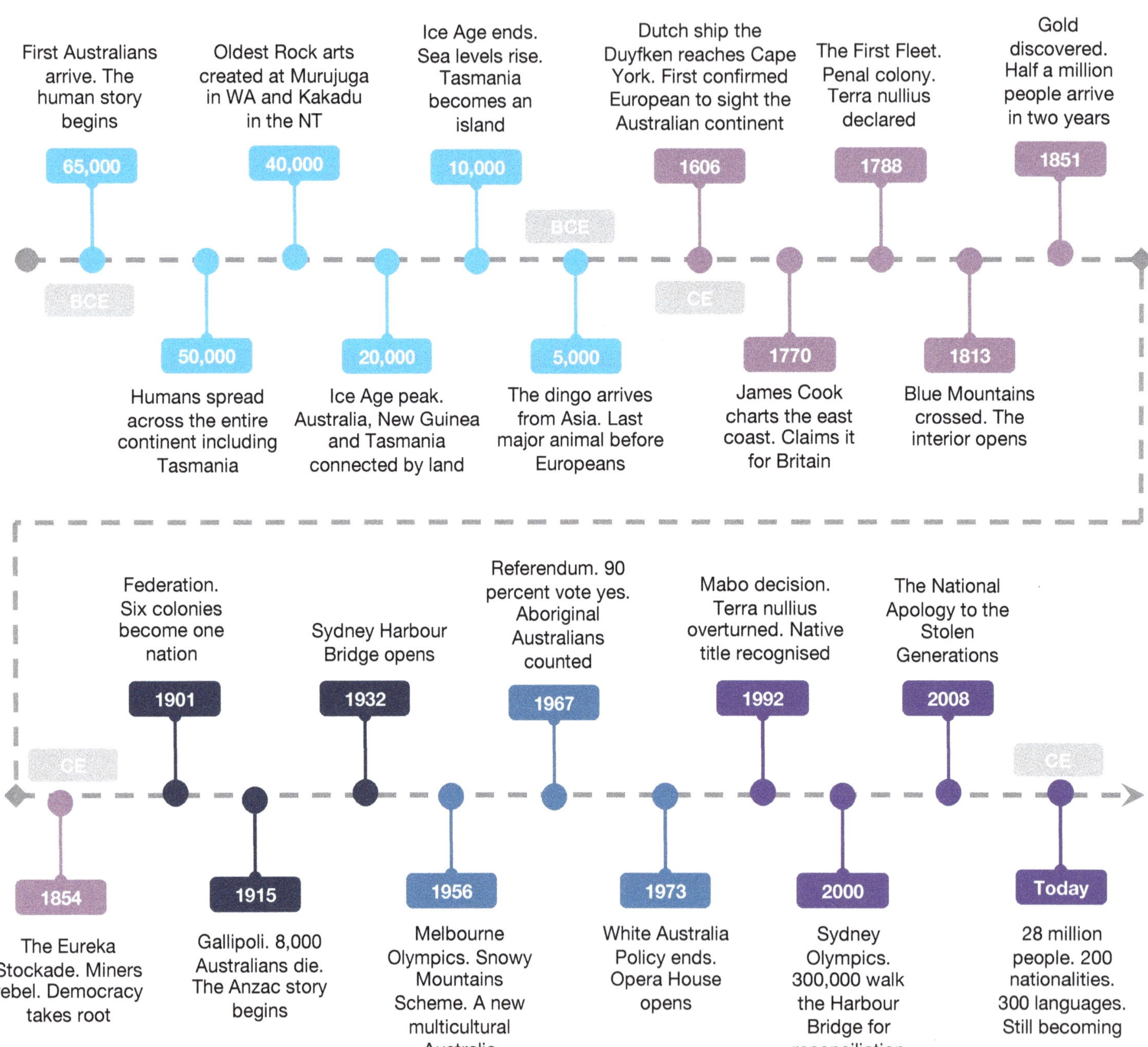

Australia in Numbers

28 million The population of Australia. Roughly the same as the state of Texas, spread across a continent the size of the contiguous United States.

86% The proportion of Australians who live in cities, mostly in a narrow coastal strip. One of the most urbanised countries on Earth, despite having one of the most dramatic interiors.

7.7 million sqkm The total area of Australia. The sixth largest country on Earth. Drive across it and you will travel further than London to Mumbai.

32% The proportion of Australian residents born overseas. Among the highest in the world. More than 200 nationalities are represented in the Australian population.

300+ The number of languages spoken in Australian homes. After English, the most widely spoken languages include Mandarin, Arabic, Vietnamese, Cantonese, Punjabi and Greek.

1788 The year European settlement began. Australia as a nation is 125 years old. The cultures it was built on top of are at least 520 times older.

65,000+ The minimum number of years Aboriginal and Torres Strait Islander peoples have lived on this continent. The oldest continuous civilisations on Earth.

812K The number of Aboriginal and Torres Strait Islander Australians today, approximately 3.2 percent of the total population. There are over 500 distinct First Nations groups.

250+ The number of distinct Aboriginal language groups present before European settlement. Approximately 120 of those languages are still spoken today.

6 The number of states. Two territories. Eight capital cities. One country that sometimes feels like several.

1 The number of countries that occupy an entire continent. Every border in Australia is internal. The coastline is the only edge.

The Peoples and Nations of Australia

Before there was a country called Australia, there was a continent of nations.

For at least 65,000 years, the land now called Australia was home to over 250 distinct peoples, each with their own language, their own Country, their own law, their own knowledge systems and their own ceremonies. They were not one culture. They were as different from each other as the French are from the Finns or the Punjabis are from the Tamil. What they shared was a relationship with this continent of extraordinary depth and duration.

In the tropical north, the Yolngu people of Arnhem Land in the Northern Territory developed one of the most complex kinship systems in the world. On the south-western corner of the continent, the Noongar people of what is now Western Australia maintained a network of seasonal movement across their Country that had functioned for thousands of years. In the central desert, the Arrernte people of the Alice Springs region encoded their knowledge of a harsh landscape in ceremony and song of extraordinary precision. Along the south-eastern coast, the Eora people of the Sydney region were the first to encounter the British and the first to experience what that encounter meant.

Each of these groups had a name for their own Country. None of them had a name for the whole continent because, for them, the whole continent was not one place. It was a mosaic of Countries, each belonging to its people as much as its people belonged to it.

When the British arrived in 1788 they saw emptiness. What was actually there was complexity, variety, depth and law. The idea that this complexity was invisible to the newcomers is one of the most consequential mistakes in Australian history. Understanding that it was not emptiness but fullness is where this book begins.

The map on this page shows the broad regional groupings of First Nations peoples across the continent. It is a simplification. The reality is far more intricate. Every river system and mountain range and coastal strip has its own people and its own stories. This map is an invitation to look more closely, not a substitute for doing so.

ANCIENT COUNTRY
SIXTY-FIVE THOUSAND YEARS OF CONTINUITY
This image is an AI-generated artistic concept. The boundaries and pathways shown are fictional and do not represent actual Indigenous
language groups, territories or Songlines. For an accurate cultural map, please refer to the official AIATSIS Map of Indigenous Australia.

Advance Australia Fair

Australians all let us rejoice
For we are one and free
We've golden soil and wealth for toil
Our home is girt by sea
Our land abounds in nature's gifts
Of beauty rich and rare
In history's page let every stage
Advance Australia Fair

In joyful strains then let us sing
Advance Australia Fair

A note on the anthem - Advance Australia Fair was written by Peter Dodds McCormick in 1878. Australia adopted it as the national anthem in 1974, replacing God Save the Queen. In 1976, God Save the Queen was briefly reinstated, before Advance Australia Fair was formally proclaimed again as the national anthem in 1984. A second verse exists but is rarely sung.

For most of its history the anthem began with the words "Australians all let us rejoice, for we are young and free." In January 2021 the second word of the second line was changed by the federal government, with agreement from all state and territory governments, from "young" to "one."

The change was made in recognition of Australia's First Nations history. A country whose cultures stretch back at least 65,000 years is not young. The word "one" was chosen to reflect a nation that contains many peoples and many histories. It was the smallest possible change to the text and one of the most significant statements the country has made about itself in recent decades.

Not everyone agreed with the change. Some felt it was insufficient. Some felt it was unnecessary. The debate about the anthem, like the debate about the date of Australia Day and the debate about the republic, is really a debate about what Australia chooses to say about itself and what story it wants to tell.

The anthem is printed here in its current form, with "one and free." Whether that form will be the final one is a question only the young oldest country can answer.

ARC 1
THE DEEP FOUNDATION

What was here before Australia existed and why it still matters

01 **The Continent That Was Never Empty**
Before history began, this land was already full…

02 **The Land That Knows You**
Why Aboriginal Australians do not own the land, they belong to it..

03 **The Song and The Dream**
The oldest navigation system on Earth has no paper and no ink…

01 The Continent That Was Never Empty

School holidays. Oliver has come over to play cricket in the backyard with Arjun. Mei is there too, just back from their trip to Darwin.

Mei: We went to Kakadu. The rock paintings are tens of thousands of years old. Our ranger was from the Bininj people. He knew every image and what it meant.

Arjun: How old is tens of thousands exactly?

Dad: *(leaning on the fence)* Think about the Egyptian pyramids. Built 4,500 years ago.

Arjun: Right.

Dad: The Roman Empire lasted about 500 years. Everything humans have ever written down covers roughly 5,000 years in total.

Oliver: And Aboriginal Australians were here before all of that?

Dad: They were living here, developing languages and laws and ceremonies, for thirteen times that length. Before a single word was written anywhere on Earth.

Arjun looks at the bat in his hands for a moment.

Arjun: That is almost impossible to imagine.

Dad: That is the point.

Most countries measure their history in hundreds of years. Australia's First Nations peoples measure their continuous cultural presence in tens of thousands, making them the custodians of the oldest living cultures on Earth.

How do we know? Archaeologists dig carefully through layers of earth. The deeper they go the further back in time they reach. Objects found in the same layer can be dated using techniques that measure the decay of radioactive elements in the sediment around them. At Madjedbebe rock shelter in the Northern Territory, stone tools and ground ochre have been found in layers dating to at least 65,000 years ago. More recent genetic studies suggest the ancestors of Aboriginal Australians may have arrived as many as 75,000 years ago, making the initial migration from Africa through Asia one of the longest journeys in human prehistory.

Over those tens of thousands of years, the cultures on this continent multiplied and diversified. When sea levels rose around 12,000 years ago, Tasmania was separated from the mainland and communities that had been connected became isolated. Over thousands of years in that isolation, distinct languages and customs and knowledge systems developed independently. By the time Europeans arrived, those 250 or more language groups were not just different dialects. They were entirely distinct civilisations, as different from each other as any two cultures on Earth.

What they shared was the depth of their relationship with this land and the sophistication of the knowledge built on it across thousands of generations. That knowledge covered ecology, medicine, navigation, astronomy, law and governance. It was encoded in song and story and ceremony in ways that proved more durable than paper. It did not need to be written down. It survived because it was lived.

When a First Nations elder speaks about their Country today, they draw on a tradition not just old but continuously maintained and tested against the reality of the land. That is not heritage. That is expertise. And it is the oldest part of the young oldest country.

Voices From Country: The Yolngu people of Arnhem Land have passed down their knowledge for tens of thousands of years through stories, songs and ceremonies. These stories describe how ancestral beings travelled across the land, shaping rivers, rocks and pathways, while also helping people remember where to find water, how seasons change and how to care for Country. When researchers began listening closely in the twentieth century, they found that Yolngu traditions carried detailed ecological knowledge and observations of the sky, preserved carefully across generations, with some parts aligning with environmental evidence. As one elder explained, "Our law is not written in books. It is written in the land," meaning every place holds memory and every ceremony helps keep that knowledge alive.

02 The Land That Knows You

A Sunday afternoon. The backyard after lunch. Dad is pruning the rose bushes near the fence. Arjun comes out with a book and sits on the back step. Navya is turning over rocks nearby, looking for beetles and bugs.

Arjun: Dad, when Aboriginal people say Country, what do they actually mean?

Dad: *(not looking up)* More than land.

Arjun: What then?

Dad: Country is the whole thing. The land, the water, the sky. The plants and animals, the songs and stories, the ancestors. A living system you are part of. Not something you own.

Arjun: We own this garden though.

Dad: We have a title deed. That is different from belonging to it. Aboriginal Australians do not say they own their Country. They say they belong to it.

Navya holds up a small beetle on the end of her finger.

Navya: Is this little thing part of Country?

Dad: Yes. Everything is.

She puts it back carefully under the rock.

Arjun: Even the rocks?

Think about the place where you grew up. The street, the backyard, the park nearby. You know it well. But knowing a place and belonging to it are different things. For Aboriginal Australians, Country is not a location you know. It is a system you belong to. Country includes the land, the water, the sky above it, the plants and animals, the songs and stories and the ancestors. It is alive. It can be healthy or sick. It can miss you when you are gone.

You do not own Country. Country holds you. Every Aboriginal Australian has a Country, a specific area of land with a deep inherited relationship attached to it. That relationship is not chosen. It is given at birth, embedded in kinship and ceremony and song. You cannot lose your Country, though you can be separated from it. This is not a poetic way of talking. For Aboriginal Australians it is a precise description of how the world works. Consider fire management. Aboriginal Australians burned the land deliberately for tens of thousands of years, at the right time in the right place. That controlled burning shaped which plants grew and which animals came. It kept the country healthy and abundant. This was not instinct. It was science, developed and refined across thousands of generations of careful watching.

Country and its people are in an ongoing relationship, not a transaction. A person who cares for Country is maintaining something real. The language of Country, the ceremonies that keep it alive, the songlines that map it and the laws that govern it, are not relics of the past. They are a living system still being practiced, still being passed to children and still shaping how millions of Australians understand the land they live on.

Two words capture the whole difference. English speakers say they own land. Aboriginal Australians say they belong to Country. Owning means you are in charge of the land. Belonging means the land is part of you. You cannot sell something you belong to any more than you can sell your family. That is not a poetic distinction. It is the difference between two entirely different ways of being in the world.

Voices From Country: In the 1830s a Palawa elder from Lutruwita (Tasmania) described a star called Moinee that once sat near the south celestial pole. He drew its position in the sand, triangulating it against other stars. No such star sits near the southern pole today. Scientists were puzzled until they understood axial precession, the slow wobble of the Earth that shifts star positions over thousands of years. Calculating backwards, Moinee matched the position of the star Canopus approximately 12,000 years ago, exactly when the land bridge connecting Tasmania to the mainland was flooding. The elder was describing the night sky at the moment his ancestors watched their world become an island. The knowledge had been carried, undisturbed, for 500 generations.

03 The Song and The Dream

School holidays. The family is on a road trip to the Grampians. Navya is asleep. Dad has put on a recording of Aboriginal singing. Mum is driving. Arjun looks out at the flat plains.

Arjun: What is that music?

Dad: A song from a songline. A walking song.

Arjun: What is a songline?

Dad: Imagine crossing Australia with no GPS, no roads, no maps. You sing it. The landscape becomes the lyrics. Every hill and waterhole has a verse. Know the song, know the way.

Arjun: Does it actually work?

Dad: Scientists have verified some songs describe coastlines that disappeared ten thousand years ago. And the Dreaming connects to them too. The songs keep the ancestors alive in the land.

Navya stirs.

Navya: *(half asleep, softly singing)* Waranyjarri gunya garrjin...

Arjun: *(turning)* What is that?

Navya: We are one but we are many. We learned it at kinder when I was younger.

A pause. Then Dad starts humming. Arjun joins in. Then all three of them, quietly, in the moving car with the plains going past.

All: We are one but we are many...

Mum: *(smiling at the road ahead)* That is exactly it.

The Songlines

Imagine you need to travel across Australia. No phone, no road signs, no maps. Just you and thousands of kilometres of desert and mountain and plain between you and where you need to go. How do you find your way?

For Aboriginal Australians, the answer was song. Every feature of the landscape, every hill, waterhole, rock formation and river bend, had a name and a verse. Put the verses together and you had a route. Learn the song and you knew exactly where to walk, where to find water and when to turn.

These are called songlines. A single songline might cross the entire continent, passing through dozens of different language groups. Each group knew their section of the song. When you crossed into their Country you had to know their verses, both to navigate and to show respect.

Scientists have been amazed to discover how accurate the songlines are. Some of them describe coastlines and waterholes that no longer exist, landscapes that changed at the end of the last Ice Age over 10,000 years ago. The people who watched those coastlines disappear encoded what they saw into song and that song survived intact.

Think about what that means. These are the oldest maps on Earth. Not drawn on paper, not stored in a computer. Carried in the voice and in the memory of a community, passed from elder to child across thousands of generations.

That is also what makes songlines remarkable as a knowledge system. A book can be burned. A hard drive can be wiped. But knowledge that lives in people, passed from voice to voice across tens of thousands of years, survives as long as the community survives. The songlines have endured for tens of thousands of years. They are still being sung today.

Voices From Country: The Seven Sisters songline is one of the longest in Australia, stretching from the Pilbara across the central deserts into South Australia. It tells the story of seven ancestral women pursued across the sky and the land, with landmarks such as rock formations and waterholes woven into the journey. Different language groups hold different sections, passing the story across Country as the path continues. Researchers have found that many parts of the songline closely match real landscapes and travel routes. It is both story and system, a way of remembering, navigating and caring for Country, carried in song across generations.

The Dreaming

Here is something that takes a moment to understand.

When you learn history at school, the past is behind you. Things happened, they are over and what remains are the records and the results. The Roman Empire fell. Done. The dinosaurs died. Done. History moves in one direction.

The Dreaming does not work like that.

For Aboriginal Australians, the ancestral beings who shaped the land are not in the past. They are still present. Every mountain, river, waterhole and desert plain is the physical trace of something they did. The land is not just scenery. It is evidence. It is alive with meaning.

Ceremony is how that meaning is maintained. When the right people perform the right ceremony in the right place, they are not remembering something that happened long ago. They are keeping it alive right now. The world, in this understanding, needs that attention. Without ceremony, something real is lost.

The Dreaming is also the law. The ancestral beings established the rules for how people must live together. Who can marry whom. Who has custodianship of which songs. Who has the right to speak for which Country. These are not rules that humans invented. They are the conditions of the world as it is.

None of this is easy for someone who grew up with a Western understanding of history and religion to absorb. That is okay. The point is not to fully understand the Dreaming from the outside. The point is to understand that it is a complete and sophisticated way of understanding the world, developed over 65,000 years and that it deserves to be taken seriously on its own terms.

Voices From Country: The Warlpiri word for the Dreaming is *Jukurrpa*. It means "the Dreaming," "the Law" and "what is real" all at once, not as three different ideas but as one. Many Aboriginal scholars prefer to leave the word untranslated. As one elder explained it: "The Dreaming is not a fairy story. It is the truth of the land." When you understand that, the ceremonies make sense, the songlines make sense and the deep seriousness with which Aboriginal Australians speak about their Country makes sense.

Story - The Emu in the Sky

Aboriginal Australia, tens of thousands of years

The fire has burned to coals. The children are asleep.

An elder sits outside looking up. The Milky Way stretches from one horizon to the other, dense with stars. But she is not watching the stars. She is watching the darkness between them.

There, running across the sky, is the long neck and the rounded body and the trailing legs. The Emu in the Sky. Not made of stars but of the dark lanes of dust that cut through the galaxy, blotting the light behind them. You have to know how to look. She has known since she was younger than the children sleeping now.

She watches the Emu's posture. Tonight the head is low on the horizon just after sunset, the body stretching upward, the bird in full running stride. She nods slowly.

Tomorrow she will tell the others. The eggs are ready.

This is the calendar. Not a grid of squares on a wall, not a list of numbered days. The Emu's posture changes across the year as the Earth moves along its orbit and each position marks something. When the eggs are in the ground, when the birds are nesting, when the rains are coming, when it is time for ceremony. The sky is not decoration. It is a working document, updated every night.

The knowledge lives in her the way all knowledge lives here, in the body and in the story and in the song that was learned from the grandmother of her grandmother's grandmother. No clay tablet. No paper. No calendar hanging by a nail.

She looks at the Emu a moment longer. Then she goes inside.

On any clear autumn night in the Southern Hemisphere, if you know where to look, you can find the Emu running across the sky. The knowledge that reads it has been passed from elder to child on this continent for longer than any other calendar system on Earth has existed. It is still being passed on tonight.

04 The Morning Everything Changed

The family is in Sydney for summer holidays. They are at Circular Quay. The Opera House is to their left, the Harbour Bridge ahead. Navya is eating a gelato. Arjun looks out at the harbour.

Arjun: What did this look like before all of this was here?

Dad: Trees right to the water's edge. The Eora people had lived around this harbour for thousands of years.

Arjun: So one day ships just appeared?

Dad: Not quite. It started eighteen years earlier. A navigator called James Cook sailed this entire coast in 1770 and claimed it for Britain. He had a botanist with him called Joseph Banks.

Arjun: What did Banks do?

Dad: He wrote a report. Said the harbour was excellent and the land fertile. That report sat in London for eighteen years. Then a man called Arthur Phillip read it, loaded eleven ships and sailed halfway around the world.

Arjun: So that report is why Phillip came?

Dad: Cook found the door. Banks described what was behind it. Phillip walked through.

Arjun: Is that when the First Fleet arrived? January 26. We learned about it at school but I cannot remember the year.

Dad: Yes. January 26, 1788. Eleven ships. About 1,500 people, more than half of them convicts. Phillip anchored roughly where we are standing now.

Navya: *(looking at the water)* Did they know everything was going to change?

Dad: No one ever does.

A ferry horn sounds across the harbour.

On the morning of January 26, 1788, eleven ships anchored in what is now Sydney Harbour and the course of the Australian continent changed permanently. Captain Arthur Phillip stepped ashore and formally claimed possession of the eastern half of the continent for the British Crown.

Eighteen years earlier James Cook had sailed this coast and claimed it for Britain. His botanist Joseph Banks reported enthusiastically on the harbour and the land. It was Banks who later recommended the site to the British government as a solution to a pressing problem. Britain's prisons were overflowing. The American colonies, which had absorbed transported convicts for decades, were no longer available after their independence. A new destination was needed. Banks proposed Botany Bay. The first fleet carried 778 convicts along with marines, officials and supplies. The 1788 arrival was entirely deliberate.

The Eora people who watched from the shore had no framework for what they were seeing. They had encountered other peoples before but nothing like this. The ships were unlike anything in their experience. The men who stepped ashore wore strange clothes, carried unfamiliar objects and spoke in a language with no connection to any tongue in the region. Some Eora accounts describe the newcomers as spirits of the dead, returned in an unrecognisable form. Within weeks it was clear these were not spirits. They were people who intended to stay.

What the British did not know was that they were not arriving in a wilderness. They were arriving in a managed landscape. The grasslands they found had been shaped by tens of thousands of years of deliberate fire management. They inherited a garden and called it empty land.

January 26 is now Australia's national day. For many Aboriginal Australians it marks the beginning of something that proved deeply destructive to their world. The date is not going away but what it means is still being argued over. That argument is one of the most honest things about this country.

Everything that follows in this book follows from that morning.

Did You Know? The name Australia comes from the Latin word australis meaning southern. The continent had been called New Holland by Dutch navigators who mapped parts of the western and southern coast in the 1600s. Matthew Flinders, who completed the first circumnavigation of the continent in 1803, proposed the name Australia in his writings. It was formally adopted as the official name in 1824. For the 65,000 years before that every language group on the continent had their own name for their own Country. None of them needed a name for the whole continent because for them the whole continent was not one place.

05 Two Latin Words That Erased a Continent

A Sunday afternoon at Chadstone. Dad and Arjun are on a bench in the food court waiting for Mum and Navya. Mei is with them, eating a pretzel. Arjun has his school history book out.

Arjun: Terra nullius. Nobody's land. That is what the British called Australia when they arrived?

Dad: Officially yes. The continent legally empty. Belonging to no one.

Arjun: But there were hundreds of thousands of people here.

Dad: The legal argument was that those people did not count as occupants.

Arjun: Why not?

Dad: They did not have farms. They did not have fences. They did not have written deeds. Therefore in the eyes of British law the land was available.

Arjun: That is not a legal argument. That is just deciding the rules so you win.

Dad: *(after a pause)* Yes. That is a fair description of what happened.

Navya and Mum appear through the crowd.

Navya: What are you reading?

Arjun: About a rule somebody made up to say that nobody was here.

Navya: Can we get Boost?

Mei: *(to Arjun)* That was actually a really good summary.

Dad: The most honest one I have heard.

Arjun: *(already standing)* Let's go.

Terra nullius is Latin for "nobody's land." The British used this idea to justify taking Australia without negotiating, without paying and without declaring war. The argument was that Aboriginal Australians did not count as owners under British law. They did not have farms. They did not have fences. They did not have written title deeds. Therefore, in British legal thinking, the land was free to take.

This was wrong. The continent was plainly occupied. Aboriginal Australians had detailed systems of land ownership and boundaries that had worked for tens of thousands of years. But those systems were deliberately ignored, because recognising them would have meant negotiating rather than simply taking. The consequences were enormous. No treaty was ever signed between the British Crown and Aboriginal peoples. Australia is one of the very few colonised countries in the world where this never happened. The land was declared available. Everything that followed was built on that declaration.

For over a century this remained the legal foundation of Australia. Governments passed laws controlling where Aboriginal people could live, work and move, often without consent or negotiation. Terra nullius had made this possible by making the original owners invisible in law.

The overturning of terra nullius came in 1992. The Mabo decision forced the legal system to acknowledge that another system of law had existed here continuously, before and during and after British settlement. Native title is not a gift from the Australian government. It is the recognition of something that was always there.

Since 1992, Australia has been trying, imperfectly and slowly, to reckon with what terra nullius made possible. Native title claims have been recognised across more than three million square kilometres of the continent. A formal apology was delivered in 2008 to the Stolen Generations. In 2017 First Nations leaders gathered at Uluru and issued a document calling for a Voice to Parliament, a truth-telling process and a treaty. The conversation that terra nullius tried to prevent is finally, beginning.

Worth Knowing: In 1967, Australians voted in a national referendum to include Aboriginal and Torres Strait Islander peoples in the national census and to allow the federal government to make laws for them. The "yes" vote was 90.77 percent, the highest approval of any referendum in Australian history. Until this referendum, Aboriginal Australians were excluded from official population counts for constitutional purposes. The referendum removed that exclusion and enabled the federal government to legislate on their behalf. The fact that this required a referendum at all reflects how deeply terra nullius had shaped the law. The fact that nine in ten Australians voted to change it reflects something else.

06 The Two Ideas That Could Never Coexist

A Saturday afternoon. Dad and Arjun are driving through a new suburb on the eastern fringe of Melbourne. Street after street of new houses, small blocks, concrete driveways.

Arjun: Dad, what was here before all of this?

Dad: Farmland. Before that grassland. Before that Country.

Arjun: And now every square metre is owned by someone.

Dad: That is a very specific idea about what land is.

Arjun: What idea?

Dad: That land is property. Something you can own and sell and fence off.

Arjun: And the Aboriginal idea?

Dad: Completely different. Country cannot be owned. It can only be belonged to. Those two ideas cannot share the same legal system without one of them losing.

Arjun: And which one lost?

Dad: That is what the last two hundred years have been about.

They drive on. Every house the same. Every block bounded by a fence.

Navya: *(looking out the window)* Who lived here before the fences?

Dad: That is the question.

Two ideas about land met in Australia in 1788 and have never been fully reconciled. One said land is Country, a living system you belong to and care for. The other said land is property, something you can measure, own and sell. The British brought the second idea. Turning Country into property required a specific set of tools.

To turn Country into property required several steps. First came survey, measuring and dividing the land into parcels. Then title, legal documents declaring who owned each parcel. Then law, courts and if necessary, force to back those documents up.

This process rolled across Australia through the nineteenth century. Land that had been managed as Country for thousands of years was divided up and handed to settlers.

The survey chain became one of the most powerful instruments of colonisation. Surveyors moved ahead of settlement, measuring and pegging out parcels of land. The act of measurement was the act of possession. Once a line was drawn on a map and a peg driven into the ground, the land became a legal object. It could be granted, sold, mortgaged and inherited.

The people who had lived on it had no role in this process. They were not consulted. Their existing boundaries, maintained for thousands of years through song and ceremony and law, were invisible to the surveyor's chain.

For Aboriginal peoples, watching this happen to their Country was not simply a loss of land. It was the imposition of an entirely foreign way of understanding the world. The idea that a stranger could arrive, measure a piece of your Country and declare it theirs by writing numbers in a book was not just unjust. It was incomprehensible. The two systems of law had no common ground.

The collision between these two ideas has never been resolved. Every native title claim in Australian courts, every planning dispute where Aboriginal cultural heritage is weighed against a development proposal, is this argument continuing. Two entirely different ideas about what land is, sitting together in the same legal system, still unresolved.

Worth Knowing: Over three million square kilometres of Australia is now subject to native title claims or determinations. That is more than the entire area of India. It represents the ongoing legal recognition that for large parts of this continent the idea of land as property introduced by the British has never fully replaced the prior idea of land as Country. The argument that began on a harbour shore in 1788 is still being resolved in courtrooms and on Country today.

07 The War That Was Never Called a War

School holidays. Arjun and Oliver are playing backyard cricket. Dad is reading nearby. They take a break and come inside for water.

Oliver: Hey, my nan has this old photo. Mr Paterson's great-grandfather, standing on this massive property out past Ballarat. Like thousands of acres. Pretty cool actually.

Dad: *(looking up)* Did you know how that property became theirs?

Oliver: *(shrugging)* Nah. I just figured his family had always been there. Why?

Dad: Land like that did not just appear. There were people on it. And clearing them off was not peaceful in most parts of Australia.

Arjun: Were there actual wars here?

Dad: For over a hundred years across the continent. Not called wars in most history books. But that is what they were.

Oliver: Why did no one tell me at school?

Dad: Because for most of Australia's history it was easier not to talk about it. If you admit there were wars you have to admit there were people with rights worth fighting for.

Arjun turns the cricket bat over in his hands.

Arjun: And we have not finished reckoning.

Dad: Not even close.

The War That Was Never Named

For most of the nineteenth century, armed conflict between Aboriginal peoples and European settlers spread across the continent. It followed the advancing frontier, moving inland from the coast as settlers pushed further into the interior. It was not a single declared war with a clear beginning or end. It was decades of localised violence that was never formally named by governments and never concluded by treaty.

The central driver was access to land and water. Settlers moved into areas already occupied, used and managed by Aboriginal peoples, and conflict often followed. Colonial governments did not remain neutral. They generally supported settler expansion, deploying police forces and, at times, organised armed groups. Punitive expeditions were carried out to remove Aboriginal communities from land sought by pastoralists. These actions were often sanctioned by authorities, even if not always formally defined as uniform policy.

The Wool Economy and the Squatters

The engine behind this expansion was wool. From the 1820s, Australia became a major supplier to British textile mills. Wool production required vast tracts of land, and after the Crossing of the Blue Mountains opened access to the interior, pastoralists moved in rapidly.

Squatters were settlers who occupied Crown land without formal purchase or survey, running sheep and cattle ahead of official settlement. Many built immense wealth. Over time, colonial governments legalised much of this occupation through leases, granting recognition to land that had been taken without agreement. The squatter became a defining figure of colonial Australia, their success tied closely to this system.

These pastoral runs spread deep into Country that Aboriginal peoples had managed for thousands of years. The wool boom and the frontier conflict were not separate stories. They were deeply connected, part of the same process seen from different sides.

True Story: The Native Police - The Queensland Native Police operated from the 1840s to around 1900 as a mounted force made up of Aboriginal troopers commanded by European officers, tasked with "opening up" frontier regions for settlement, often through violent confrontation with Aboriginal communities. Historians estimate it was involved in large scale frontier killings across Queensland and northern New South Wales, likely in the thousands though exact numbers cannot be confirmed. It operated with government funding and oversight, and its records exist in official archives, many of which remain only partially studied.

The Toll

The death toll on the Aboriginal side was catastrophic. Historians estimate that tens of thousands were killed in frontier violence across the continent. The population declined sharply in the century after European arrival, due to a combination of violence, disease and displacement. In some regions, whole language groups were lost within a few generations. The scale of the loss was immense, though it was rarely named as such at the time.

The loss was not only of people. When a language group disappears, everything carried in that language is at risk. Ecological knowledge, songlines, law and stories of Country built over countless generations. In a short span of time, knowledge systems that had endured major environmental changes were broken or lost. Some of this knowledge is now being carefully recovered, but much of it cannot be rebuilt.

The Language of Silence

The violence was real. The language used to describe it often softened it. Colonial records used words like "dispersal," "encounter" and "skirmish," while the word massacre appeared less often. These terms could mask the scale and nature of what had occurred, shaping how events were recorded and remembered.

For much of Australia's modern history, this past was not widely taught, commemorated or included in the national story. The silence made it easier to avoid difficult questions about how the country was formed. Families on all sides carried these histories, often without space to speak about them openly.

That is beginning to change. The Yoorrook Justice Commission, established in 2021, is the first formal state based truth telling process of its kind in Australia. Oral histories are being recorded and massacre sites are being documented. The reckoning is slow, but it is underway.

True Story: Myall Creek - The Myall Creek Massacre in 1838 saw around 28 unarmed Aboriginal people killed by stockmen in New South Wales, and it became one of the rare frontier cases where prosecutions led to convictions and seven men were executed. A memorial established at Myall Creek in 2000 now marks the site and acknowledges the violence, standing out in a landscape where most frontier killings were never formally recorded, prosecuted or remembered.

08 The Punishment That Became a Badge of Pride

School holidays. The family is at Melbourne Museum in the Melbourne Story gallery. Everyone is reading different panels. Navya has gone ahead to the next display case.

Arjun: *(reading a panel)* So Melbourne started as a place you got sent to as punishment.

Dad: Not just Melbourne. The whole colony. Britain had overflowing prisons. Australia was the solution.

Arjun: And now having a convict ancestor is almost a badge of pride?

Dad: For many Australians yes. It became the underdog story. People who were pushed down and survived.

Navya has wandered ahead and stopped in front of a display case.

Navya: Dad. What is this armour made of?

Dad: *(walking over)* Iron. That is Ned Kelly's armour.

Navya: It is very cool.

Arjun: *(catching up)* It actually is.

Navya: If I was going to be in trouble I would want armour.

Arjun: That is not quite the lesson here, Navya.

Navya: It is a little bit the lesson.

Between 1788 and 1868 approximately 162,000 convicted men and women were transported from Britain to Australia. Britain's prisons were dangerously overcrowded. The solution for decades had been hulk ships, decommissioned vessels moored in rivers where prisoners lived in appalling conditions. When even these became unmanageable, transportation to a distant colony offered a radical answer. Remove the problem entirely. Send it to the other side of the world. Many of those transported had committed crimes of poverty, stealing food, forging documents, poaching. The sentence was transportation for seven years, fourteen years, or life.

Once here, convicts built the roads and bridges and public buildings of the colony. They were assigned as labourers and punished for infractions. When their sentences were served they became free settlers, the first generation of Australians defined by settlement rather than by punishment. For much of Australia's history convict ancestry was a source of shame. Families hid it. Records were lost deliberately or otherwise. The convict stain, as it was called, was considered a mark of inferior origins.

Then something shifted. Through the twentieth century and accelerating in the twenty-first, convict ancestry became a source of pride for many Australians. The convict story was recast as a story of ordinary people surviving an unjust system. The defiance, the irreverence and the suspicion of authority that characterised convict culture became part of the Australian national character. The stain was reimagined as a foundation. What the convict era left behind, beyond the roads and buildings, was a particular attitude toward authority. The law had been used as a weapon against ordinary people. That suspicion runs through Australian culture still, from Ned Kelly to a persistent wariness of institutions and those who run them.

The convict era ended in 1868 when the last transport ship docked in Western Australia. By then Australia had begun thinking of itself as a free settler society. But the convicts had arrived first and built the foundations. The country's oldest families are their descendants. That is not a stain. That is a beginning.

True Story: Ned Kelly - was born in 1854 to an Irish convict father and grew up poor in rural Victoria. After years of conflict with the police he turned outlaw. In 1878 he and his gang killed three policemen and became the most wanted men in Australia. His defining act was the armour he made from ploughshares, thick iron plates covering his torso and head. At the siege of Glenrowan in 1880 he walked toward police fire in that armour before being shot in the legs and captured. He was hanged in Melbourne that same year, aged 25. Australians have argued about him ever since. Was he a murderer or a rebel? A criminal or a man the system drove to it? The argument has never been settled. That, perhaps, is why he endures.

09 The Rush That Built a Democracy

A family trip to Ballarat. They are at Sovereign Hill. Mum takes Navya to try gold panning. Dad and Arjun are at a display about the Eureka Rebellion.

Arjun: Were the miners really angry enough to fight the government?

Dad: They built a stockade, sewed a flag and died for it.

Arjun: Over a mining licence?

Dad: The licence was just the surface of it. They had no vote. They had no say in how the colony was run. They paid taxes to a government that treated them like subjects, not citizens. The licence was just the thing that finally broke their patience.

Arjun: And they were not quiet.

Dad: They fought hard. Outnumbered, outgunned, but they held the stockade through the night. When the troopers charged at dawn the miners did not run.

Arjun: And?

Dad: The stockade fell in fifteen minutes. They lost the battle.

Arjun: But?

Dad: Within a year the licence was abolished. The men charged with treason were acquitted. They lost the fight but won the argument.

Arjun: So they lost but won.

Dad: That is very Australian.

Navya comes running back with a tiny vial of gold dust.

Navya: I found gold!

Dad: *(smiling)* The tradition continues.

The discovery of gold in New South Wales in 1851 transformed Australia within months. Over half a million people arrived within two years from Britain, Ireland, China and the United States. Victoria's population increased tenfold in a decade.

The scale of the find was extraordinary. In the 1850s, Victoria produced more than a third of the world's gold supply, roughly 80 tonnes a year at its peak. Tent cities appeared overnight in the bush. Ballarat and Bendigo grew from nothing into substantial towns within months. Melbourne became one of the grandest cities in the southern hemisphere, its wealth visible in the grand public buildings and civic confidence it carries to this day.

But the gold rush was not only about gold. It brought an enormous and diverse population to a colony that had been run entirely for the benefit of a small colonial establishment. Miners paid taxes to a government that gave them no vote and no say. That imbalance could not hold. The Eureka Stockade of 1854 was where it broke. Miners at Ballarat, furious at a licence fee payable whether or not they found gold, built a stockade and swore an oath to stand by one another. On December 3, soldiers charged. The battle lasted fifteen minutes. More than twenty miners were killed.

But the ideas they died for survived. Within a year the licence was abolished and the men charged with treason were acquitted. The colony began moving toward democracy. The Southern Cross flag still appears on protests today. Look up at Eureka Tower in Melbourne's Southbank and the whole story is written on the building. Blue glass for the stockade flag. A gold crown for the gold rush. A deep red band near the top for the blood spilt on that December morning. The demand for a fair go built itself into the skyline.

The gold rush also transformed the ethnic composition of Australia permanently. The Chinese communities that formed on the Victorian and New South Wales goldfields were the beginning of a Chinese Australian presence that has continued and grown for 170 years. Modern Australia was not built by the British alone. It was built by everyone who came chasing the same thing.

Around the World: The Ballarat goldfields were among the most ethnically diverse places in the world in the 1850s. Chinese miners came in large numbers and faced particular persecution including special taxes and restrictions on where they could dig. The Lambing Flat riots of 1861 in New South Wales, in which Chinese miners were attacked and driven off their claims, led directly to the first explicitly racial immigration restrictions in Australian colonial law. It was a preview of what would become the White Australia Policy forty years later.

Story - Peter Lalor at the Stockade

Ballarat, Victoria · December 3 1854

It is not yet dawn and Peter Lalor is listening.

He became the miners' leader almost by accident. He is twenty-seven, an Irish engineer three years out of Dublin. Two weeks ago he stood on a platform at Bakery Hill and called for men to stand together or be broken separately. Fifteen hundred men cheered. He did not entirely expect that.

The stockade around him is rough timber and upturned carts. Inside it, perhaps two hundred men sleep in the dark. Many more have slipped away in the night. The ones who remain know that something is coming. The troopers have been massing. The government has been patient long enough.

What they want is not complicated. They pay a licence fee to dig for gold regardless of whether they find any. They have no vote. They have no representation. They are taxed and policed and treated as subjects rather than citizens. Lalor has heard this argument in Ireland his whole life, dressed in different clothes.

He walks the perimeter of the stockade. The Southern Cross flag hangs above him in the still air, five white stars on blue. They sewed it themselves. They swore an oath beneath it. He recites the words in his head. We swear by the Southern Cross to stand truly by each other and fight to defend our rights and liberties.

There is movement near the troopers' camp. A lantern moving. Then another.

He has perhaps ten minutes. He does not run. He walks back to the centre of the stockade and begins to wake the sleeping men. His voice is quiet. He does not want panic. What he wants is for these men to know what is coming and to choose.

The troopers charge at dawn. The battle lasts fifteen minutes. Lalor loses his arm to a bullet and is carried from the field by his men. He survives. The stockade falls. But the argument the miners made that morning does not fall with it.

The Southern Cross they flew that morning still appears on protest banners across Australia today. Every time an Australian insists on their right to a say, something of Eureka is in the room.

ARC 3
THE FAULTLINES

The ideas that built a fair nation, and the cracks beneath it

10 The Deal That Made a Nation

Mei has just come back from a school trip to Canberra. She is in the backyard with Arjun and Dad.

Mei: Parliament House is enormous. It goes underground. And when you walk in the first thing you see is a huge mosaic on the floor by an Aboriginal artist. Our guide said it represents a meeting place.

Arjun: A building that runs the country and the first thing inside is an Aboriginal meeting place.

Dad: That is Australia. Old and new in the same building.

Arjun: Why is Canberra the capital? Why not Sydney or Melbourne?

Dad: Because Sydney and Melbourne could not agree. So they built a new city between them.

Mei: Our guide said the whole federation worked like that. Six colonies that had been rivals, all making deals to become one country.

Dad: In 1901 they voted to become one. The deals they made then still shape the country today.

Mei: She also said the republic debate is the same question continuing. Whether Australia has finished becoming itself.

Dad: Your guide was right.

In 1901 Australia did not exist. There were six separate British colonies, each with its own government, its own laws and its own customs duties. If you sent goods from Melbourne to Sydney you paid a tariff at the border, as if crossing into a foreign country. The idea of one Australian nation was not obvious or inevitable. It took decades of argument, negotiation and carefully managed compromise to make it happen.

The resulting constitution was a series of compromises and agreements. Every state, big or small, got equal votes in the Senate. Seats in the lower house, called the House of Representatives, were based on population. A new High Court would settle legal disputes between states. And the national government would control defence, foreign policy and customs.

What was left out is just as important. Aboriginal Australians were not recognised as citizens, were not included in the census and were largely excluded from the powers of the new federal system. The nation was formed under the legal assumption of terra nullius and carried that assumption into its founding structure.

Even the location of the capital became a compromise between rival colonies. Sydney and Melbourne both claimed the right to be the centre of the new nation, and neither would concede. The solution was to create a new city between them. Canberra did not exist before federation required it. The constitution placed it within New South Wales but at least 100 miles from Sydney, a condition driven by Victoria. An American architect, Walter Burley Griffin, won the design competition, and the city was planned in full before a single building was built.

Over time, the symbols of the nation began to reflect what had been excluded at its founding. In Parliament House, the first thing visitors see is a large mosaic designed by Michael Nelson Jagamara, a Warlpiri artist from Yuendumu. It depicts a gathering place where different groups come together to meet and talk. Installed in 1988 during the bicentenary, it stands inside a building that governs the country, but begins with an image of the cultures that were not part of its original design. That is not a full reckoning. But it is a beginning.

Worth Knowing: Australia's head of state is still the British monarch. In a 1999 referendum Australians voted against becoming a republic, partly because republicans could not agree on which model to adopt. The debate has never ended. Supporters argue that a country with 65,000 years of First Nations history and 200 years of migration from every corner of the world should not have a foreign monarch as its symbolic head. The question underneath is the same one this book keeps asking. Has Australia finished becoming itself?

11 The First Law The New Nation Passed

An evening at home. Arjun is doing history homework at the kitchen table. Mum and Dad are also at the table. Navya is watching TV.

Arjun: *(looking up)* Dad. Do you know what one of the very first laws passed by the new Australian parliament was?

Dad: Tell me.

Arjun: The Immigration Restriction Act. 1901. First session ever. Its whole purpose was to stop non-white people from entering Australia.

Dad: *(putting his book down)* Yes.

Arjun: They had just become a country. One day old as a nation. And that was the first thing they decided to do.

Dad: The mechanism was a dictation test. An officer could test an arriving migrant in any European language, even one the person had never heard. If you failed you were deported.

Arjun: So they could always make you fail.

Dad: That was the point. It was popular. Bipartisan. The mainstream view of the country's founders.

Arjun: How long did it last?

Dad: The last remnants were not officially gone until 1973.

Navya: *(comes in from the lounge)* That is seventy-two years. That is longer than Baba's age.

A pause around the table.

A young nation passed one of its first major laws with a clear idea of who it wanted to be. The White Australia Policy lasted, in various forms, for over seventy years. It was not a single law but a collection of policies and attitudes that together sought to keep Australia white. The Immigration Restriction Act of 1901 was its cornerstone. The dictation test it established allowed immigration officers to administer a test in any European language to any arriving migrant. Non-white migrants could be tested in a language they had never heard and deported when they inevitably failed. It was not designed to assess language ability. It was designed to exclude.

The policy was not marginal. It was widely supported across major political parties and defended as essential to nation building. The first Prime Minister Edmund Barton described it as necessary to preserve "a united, pure and noble Australia." It reflected the then dominant national view.

The policy reveals how national identity can be built by exclusion. Australia defined what it was by defining what it would not allow. What is unusual is how explicitly it was encoded in law and how rapidly the country subsequently transformed into something almost exactly opposite. Australians who were born under the White Australia Policy are still alive. Their children and grandchildren live in the country that policy tried to prevent from existing.

The seeds of the policy's undoing were planted almost as soon as it began. After the Second World War, Australia needed people. Under the slogan "populate or perish," Immigration Minister Arthur Calwell launched a massive migration program. When enough British migrants could not be found it opened to non-British Europeans, then gradually further. Each step made the next easier. The policy foundational in 1901 was abolished by 1973.

What replaced it is one of the most remarkable transformations any country has made. Today approximately 30 percent of Australians were born overseas. More than 200 nationalities are represented in the population. Melbourne has one of the largest Greek community outside Greece. Sydney is among the most diverse cities on Earth. The food, the music, the culture of every Australian city has been remade by people who arrived from every corner of the world and stayed and built something. The country the White Australia Policy tried to prevent from existing is the country Australia actually became. And by almost any measure, it is far better for it.

Worth Knowing: The dictation test was used as late as 1934 against Egon Kisch, a Czech journalist whose presence in Australia the government wanted to prevent. When Kisch passed tests in French and German and Italian, officials administered the test in Scottish Gaelic, a language almost no one alive spoke fluently. He failed. The case went to the High Court, which ruled the Gaelic test invalid. Kisch stayed. The episode illustrated exactly how the test was designed to work and exactly what the policy was really about.

12 The Idea That Comes With a Warning

A Saturday in winter. Dad, Arjun and Oliver are on the packed tram home after an AFL game. The crowd is still buzzing.

Oliver: Did you see that interview after the game? He kicked six goals. Six. And all he kept saying was "the boys did well today" and "we executed the game plan."

Arjun: He barely mentioned himself at all.

Oliver: It was almost strange. In any other sport the best player would be talking about himself the whole time.

Dad: That is mateship. In Australia the group matters more than the individual. Your mate is the person who shows up for you. Who does not leave you behind.

Arjun: Where does that come from?

Dad: The goldfields. The bush. The trenches. Situations where the person beside you was the difference between surviving and not.

Oliver: That is actually a beautiful idea.

Dad: You can still see it. The moment a disaster hits and the neighbours show up with food before anyone asks.

The tram rocks. The man beside them quietly helps an older woman lift her bag without being asked.

Arjun: *(watching him)* Like that.

Dad: Exactly like that.

Imagine you are on a goldfield in 1854. It is dangerous, dirty work. No health and safety rules. No hospitals nearby. The person digging next to you is the only one who will pull you out if the shaft collapses. You did not necessarily choose them. You did not know their history or their family or where they came from. None of that mattered. They were beside you in the dark. That was enough.

That is what "mate" meant originally. Not just a friend. The person who would not leave you behind. The person who would share their food when you had none and cover your back when things go wrong. The bond was not sentimental. It was practical. In conditions where everything could go wrong at any moment, the person next to you was your only insurance. Looking after them was the same as looking after yourself. Over time that practical loyalty became something deeper. A value. A way of being Australian. Mateship became one of the deepest values in Australian culture. It does not care about class or background. It is built on shared hardship and expressed through action, not words. The Anzac stories are full of it. Soldiers going back under fire to retrieve their mates. That is the image Australia built its identity around.

Mateship also has a shadow side, though a much lighter one. In a culture built on equality, someone who rises too visibly above the group can attract gentle deflation. Australians call it the tall poppy. Not a cruel thing, usually. More of a cultural reflex. Get a bit too proud of yourself and someone will find a way to bring you back to earth with a smile. It is why Australian humour is so self-deprecating. It is why successful Australians tend to underplay their achievements rather than announce them. The instinct is the same as mateship, just running in reverse. Look after the person beside you. And remember you are not better than them.

What is remarkable about mateship is how durable it has proved. It was forged in the harshest conditions the continent could produce but it never stayed there. The idea travelled out of the goldfields and the trenches and into everyday Australian life. You see it when a community rallies after a flood or a fire, when a stranger helps without being asked, when a team plays for each other rather than for individual glory. It is not a policy or a law. It is a habit of the heart. And it may be the most distinctly Australian thing there is.

True Story: In January 2011 catastrophic floods swept through Brisbane and surrounding Queensland towns. Tens of thousands of homes were inundated. Before any government recovery program was organised, something else happened. Thirty thousand volunteers simply showed up. They called themselves The Mud Army. They knocked on strangers' doors, picked up shovels and spent days hauling ruined furniture and digging mud out of houses that did not belong to them. Nobody asked them to come. Nobody paid them. They came because someone needed help and that was enough. Mateship does not wait to be organised.

13 The Two Words That Built a Welfare State

A Sunday afternoon. Oliver and Mei's families have come over for a barbecue. Both families are in the backyard. Dad is at the grill. Mum has made a vegetarian spread. The adults are talking about housing prices in Sydney and Melbourne.

Arjun: What does "fair go" actually mean?

Mei: My mum uses that phrase all the time. She says Australia gave her family a fair go when they arrived.

Arjun: But what does it actually mean?

Dad: It is the idea that everyone deserves an equal chance. Regardless of where you started. Who your parents are. What accent you have.

Oliver: Most countries say that though.

Dad: Most countries say it. Australia built it into institutions. The minimum wage. The eight-hour working day. Medicare. The fair go was not just a slogan. For most of Australian history it was backed by actual policy.

Mum: The question now is whether it still delivers. Young people in Sydney and Melbourne cannot afford to buy a house near where they work.

Mei: My parents came for that fair go. They still worry it is getting harder to find.

Navya: A fair go means I get the same dessert as Arjun.

Arjun: That is not what it means.

Navya: It is to me.

"A fair go" is probably the most Australian phrase in the English language. Every person, regardless of background, deserves a genuine opportunity to succeed. Not a guarantee of success. Not equality of outcome. Just a genuine chance. That distinction matters. The fair go was never about making everything equal. It was about making sure the starting line was not rigged.

The phrase came from the goldfields and the labour movement. In Britain, class determined everything. Your father's position, your accent, the school you attended. These notions fixed your life before it even began. In early Australia, on the chaotic goldfields where a lucky strike could make a nobody into a somebody overnight, the old hierarchies made less sense. What you did and how you treated people counted more than who your parents were.

The labour movement turned this instinct into political demands. The eight-hour working day, achieved in Melbourne in 1856 before any country in the world, and the minimum wage were expressions of the fair go principle. Ordinary workers deserved a decent standard of living not as charity but as a right.

Australia's welfare state built on this foundation. The age pension came in 1909. Unemployment benefits followed. Universal healthcare through Medicare arrived in 1975. Each was an attempt to make sure that bad luck or disadvantage did not permanently exclude someone from a decent life. Whether those institutions still deliver the fair go they were built to provide is the defining argument of modern Australian life. For decades, the 'starting line' was kept level by high wages and accessible services. But today, a new faultline has emerged. In the streets of Sydney and Melbourne, the 'Fair Go' is being tested by a housing market that feels like a closed door to the young.

The fair go also travels. Migrants who came to Australia often describe the fair go as one of the things that drew them. The idea that where you came from matters less than what you do with the opportunities in front of you. Whether Australia has always lived up to that promise is a separate question. That the promise was made, and that people believed it enough to build institutions around it, shaped the kind of country Australia became.

The Number: In 1856, building workers in Melbourne downed tools and marched from the university to Parliament House demanding an eight-hour working day. They won. Before any country in the world had done it, Melbourne's workers had established that you could not be made to work more than eight hours a day. Their slogan was simple: eight hours labour, eight hours recreation, eight hours rest. Every Australian who leaves work at five o'clock is living inside an argument those workers won on a Melbourne street 170 years ago.

14 The Country That Built Fairness Into Law

A weekday afternoon in the school holidays. Arjun has come back from the doctor with Mum. Navya has a mild fever and is on the couch. Dad is home already and puts the kettle on.

Arjun: That was so easy. We just walked in, saw the doctor, walked out. No forms, no payment, nothing.

Mum: Medicare. The government pays the doctor directly.

Arjun: Do all countries have that?

Dad: No. Most countries you pay, or you have insurance, or you go without.

Arjun: When did Australia get it?

Dad: Gough Whitlam introduced it in 1975. The idea was simple. You should not have to be rich to see a doctor.

Arjun: And before 1975?

Dad: You paid. Or you did not go.

Navya: *(from the couch, wrapped in a blanket)* I am very glad Medicare happened.

Dad: So is everyone.

Australia was among the first countries to begin building fairness into its institutions at a national level. At a time when many industrial nations still had limited or uneven welfare systems, Australia began to legislate protections. Not because it was the richest country or had a long radical tradition, but because a growing belief took hold that where you started in life should not fully determine where you ended up.

The Safety Net

In the late 1800s, if you became sick in many countries you either paid a doctor or went without treatment. If you grew old and could no longer work, support came from family or charity rather than the state. Safety nets were limited and inconsistent. Australia began building them earlier and more systematically than many comparable nations.

The age pension was introduced in 1909, recognising that people who had worked their lives should not fall into destitution in old age. The debate was intense. Opponents warned it would be too costly and discourage work. Supporters argued that abandoning the elderly undermined basic social responsibility. The proposal passed, making Australia one of the early countries to establish a government funded pension as a right rather than charity.

Unemployment support followed, along with the idea of a basic wage. The Harvester Judgment ruled that workers should earn enough to support a basic standard of living regardless of market wages. Justice Henry Bournes Higgins calculated this using the cost of food, housing and clothing for a family. This became the foundation of Australia's wage system for decades.

The First to Say Yes

Women gained federal voting rights in 1902, making Australia one of the first countries to do so at a national level. It was also the first nation to grant women both the right to vote and to stand for federal parliament. However, these rights did not apply equally to all women, with many First Nations women and non-European residents excluded under the laws of the time. Voting was one step, but participation in lawmaking was the next.

The first woman elected to an Australian parliament was Edith Cowan in Western Australia in 1921. At a time when women in many countries were still fighting for political recognition, Australian women were already entering legislatures and shaping policy.

Worth Knowing: Australia was also among the first countries to pay its members of parliament a salary, beginning in Victoria in 1870. If only wealthy people could afford to serve, parliament would only represent wealthy people. Paying MPs was the fair go principle applied to democracy.

Won, Not Given

None of these achievements arrived without a fight. The age pension was passed after years of pressure from the labour movement. The basic wage emerged from a court decision rather than employer generosity. Every gain was contested by governments, industries and institutions that resisted the cost. The fair society was built argument by argument, vote by vote. What stands out is how early Australia moved in some of these areas, compared with many other industrial nations at the time, where such systems were still emerging or uneven.

A Card and a Doctor

Gough Whitlam introduced Medibank in 1975, Australia's first universal public healthcare system. It later evolved into Medicare, which was established in its current form in 1984. The idea was simple. Access to a doctor should not depend on wealth. It was strongly opposed by sections of the medical profession, who feared control over fees, and by conservative governments who argued it would be too expensive. The system went through major political reversals before being stabilised in its modern form.

Once established, something shifted. Medicare became one of the most widely used public systems in the country. Today it funds hundreds of millions of medical services each year. No one is excluded from essential medical care because they cannot pay at the point of service. For most Australians born after its introduction, it feels normal. That is how successful institutions behave. They stop being seen as achievements and become part of the background.

What Connects Them

Every one of these systems rests on the same idea. That where you are born, who your parents are, or whether you fall sick should not determine the shape of your entire life. That a society should place a floor beneath which people cannot fall. Australia built parts of that floor earlier than many comparable countries, not because it was perfect, but because sustained political pressure made it possible. It reflects a political culture shaped by early labour movements and democratic reform, willing at key moments to use the state to enforce fairness rather than leave it to chance.

Worth Knowing: Gough Whitlam, who introduced Medicare in 1975, was dismissed as Prime Minister by the Governor-General later that same year in the most dramatic constitutional crisis in Australian history. His government had run into conflict with the Senate over supply. The dismissal remains deeply controversial. But the institutions Whitlam built, Medicare, university free education and the arts funding model, survived him and became permanent features of Australian life. He lost power. His legacy did not.

Story - The Tunnel Breaks Through

Snowy Mountains, New South Wales · 1956

Modesto Correale does not think about Italy today. That is unusual.

He has been in Australia for three years, working on the Snowy Mountains Hydroelectric Scheme in tunnels through granite in the highest mountains on the continent. The work is the hardest he has ever done. The cold is different from the cold he knew in Calabria. The mountains are different. Everything is different.

But today is holing through day on his section. Two teams have been drilling from opposite ends of the tunnel for fourteen months. Today they will meet in the middle. If the surveyors have done their work correctly, if the drilling has held its line through fourteen months of granite and darkness, the two faces will align within centimetres of each other. He is three hundred metres inside the mountain. The air smells of rock dust and diesel and the particular cold that lives underground. His team is at the face. The drill is running. And somewhere beyond this wall of rock, coming toward him through the same mountain from the other side, is another team he has never met.

He thinks about the men on the other side. Poles, most of them, he has been told. Men who left their country the same way he left his. Men who came to this continent because it offered something their own countries could not. They speak different languages. They eat different food. They pray differently or not at all. In fourteen months of drilling toward each other through a mountain in the Australian alps they have not yet exchanged a single word.

The drill stops. Silence. Then, from the other side of the rock face, faintly, the sound of drilling. Getting louder. His foreman turns to him and grins. The gap is a metre. Maybe less. He picks up his drill.

The Snowy Mountains Hydroelectric Scheme took 25 years and over 100,000 workers from 30 countries to complete. Sixteen men died in tunnel work alone. The scheme remains one of the largest engineering projects in Australian history and one of the most deliberate acts of nation building through migration the country has ever undertaken.

The children and grandchildren of those workers are Australians now. The country they live in was partly built by the hands of their ancestors, in the highest mountains on the continent, far from home.

15 The Country That Pushes Back

A January evening. The whole family is inside because it is forty degrees. The news has bushfire reports from Queensland. Every blind is pulled down.

Navya: Why does Australia have so many disasters?

Dad: The continent is geologically old. It sits in a climate zone that produces extremes as a matter of course. Drought, flood, fire, cyclone. These are not unusual events. They are the rhythm of the place.

Arjun: And Australians just accept that?

Dad: Over time yes. You plan for the fire. You have the kit for the flood.

Mum: It shapes everything. Houses on stilts in Queensland, underground homes in Coober Pedy, fireproof materials in the south. You build for what you know is coming.

Arjun: Does it shape how people relate to each other?

Dad: When the disaster comes the mateship comes with it. Strangers helping strangers. That is when you really see it.

The thermometer on the wall reads forty-one.

Navya: Welcome to summer in Australia.

Australia is a continent of extremes. Its geological age, flat interior and position across the global desert belt combine to produce a climate operating at scales few other places on Earth experience.

The drought flood cycle of eastern Australia is among the most volatile in the world. The same river systems that flood catastrophically in La Niña years can remain dry for years during El Niño events. Rivers that become impassable torrents in one decade can turn to cracked earth in the next. In Australia, weather is not background. It is a defining force that shapes settlement, agriculture and daily life.

Bushfire is perhaps the most culturally defining feature of the Australian climate. These fires are natural in origin but their intensity today is also shaped by land management choices over the past two centuries. The Black Summer of 2019 to 2020 was the most severe fire season in recorded Australian history. Fires burned approximately 18 million hectares across New South Wales, Victoria, Queensland and South Australia, with an estimated three billion animals killed or displaced.

Beyond the immediate destruction, events like Black Summer reshape how people understand risk itself. Smoke can travel across states and reach major cities far from the fire front, making disaster something experienced indirectly but continuously. Insurance, housing design and even migration patterns respond in subtle ways to this background awareness that extremes are not rare events but recurring conditions.

A country that lives with disruption builds systems of response. The volunteer fire services, SES volunteers and neighbours who turn up after disaster reflect a repeated national pattern of informal collective action. Mateship becomes most visible not in normal times but under strain.

The relationship between climate and character is not simple cause and effect, but it is real. A country that burns and floods regularly develops a particular awareness of fragility and recovery. Disasters are not interruptions to ordinary life. They are part of it, shaping a culture that holds its possessions more lightly and its people more tightly than most.

The Numbers: 50.7 degrees Celsius is the hottest temperature ever recorded in Australia, first at Oodnadatta in South Australia in 1960 and matched at Onslow in Western Australia in 2022. 18 million hectares burned in the Black Summer fires of 2019 to 2020, an area larger than England and Wales combined. Australia holds the world record for the highest rate of mammal extinction since European settlement, with at least 30 of the roughly 300 mammal species present in 1788 now gone forever.

The same continent that burns also shelters one of the most extraordinary ecosystems on Earth. The Great Barrier Reef stretches 2,300 kilometres along the Queensland coast. It is the largest living structure on Earth, home to more than 1,500 species of fish, around 4,000 types of mollusc, 240 species of birds and six of the world's seven species of marine turtle. There is nothing else like it. It is also under severe stress.

Coral bleaching occurs when ocean temperatures rise beyond what coral can tolerate. The coral expels the algae that gives it colour and energy. Without it, the coral turns white and is more likely to die. The Great Barrier Reef has experienced several mass bleaching events since 1998. The most severe occurred in 2016 and 2017, when surveys found that large portions of shallow water coral in the northern reef were lost.

The primary driver is ocean warming linked to climate change. This creates a central tension in Australian environmental politics. Australia is one of the world's largest exporters of coal and gas. The combustion of those fuels contributes to global emissions that warm the oceans. The reef, widely regarded as a national treasure, is being affected by the same global system that much of the Australian economy depends on. The country that helps protect the reef also exports resources that contribute to its decline.

Australia has invested heavily in protecting the reef from local pressures. Fishing restrictions, water quality programs and marine park protections have all played a role in slowing damage. But local action alone cannot address a global driver. The reef cannot be preserved by Australia in isolation. Its future depends on international emissions reductions, which have been uneven and slow.

The conservation movement in Australia also connects to something deeper. The idea that some places should not be measured only by what can be extracted from them, but by what they are in themselves, has found strong support across different communities. For many First Nations Australians, this aligns with older understandings of Country as living system rather than resource. That shared perspective has helped shape one of the most influential environmental coalitions in modern Australian public life.

Worth Knowing: The Great Barrier Reef was listed as a UNESCO World Heritage Site in 1981. UNESCO has repeatedly threatened to list it as "in danger" due to bleaching and water quality. Australia has lobbied hard against this listing, arguing it would damage tourism. The argument about whether to acknowledge the reef's deterioration publicly is itself a reflection of a deeper argument about what kind of country Australia wants to be.

The Wildlife – An interlude on what lives here

Australia separated from the supercontinent Gondwana around 50 million years ago and drifted north alone. Cut off from the rest of the world, its wildlife evolved in complete isolation for tens of millions of years. The result is a catalogue of creatures found nowhere else on Earth, so strange and so beautiful that early European naturalists refused to believe what they were seeing.

The platypus was the first great shock. When a dried specimen arrived in England in 1799, the scientist examining it was convinced it was a hoax. A mammal with a duck's bill, a beaver's tail, otter's feet, that lays eggs and detects prey through electrical signals in its bill. He looked for the stitching where someone must have sewn the pieces together. There was no stitching. The platypus was real. It remains one of the most extraordinary animals on Earth and it lives in the rivers of eastern Australia.

More than 80 percent of Australia's mammals, reptiles and flowering plants exist nowhere else. The continent is a living museum of evolutionary paths not taken elsewhere. Kangaroos and wallabies, wombats and koalas, echidnas and bilbies. Many of them marsupials, all carrying their young in pouches, all shaped by millions of years of island evolution. They are not primitive versions of other animals. They are a completely different answer to the same questions of survival.

The birds are equally extraordinary. The kookaburra, whose laughing call announces dawn across the eastern bush, is the world's largest kingfisher. The rainbow lorikeet arrives in suburban gardens in flocks of riotous colour, feeding on nectar with a brush-tipped tongue. The superb lyrebird can mimic any sound it hears including chainsaws and camera shutters with perfect accuracy. The cassowary, in the rainforests of north Queensland, is one of the few birds in the world considered genuinely dangerous to humans. The emu, which cannot fly, outran European settlers on horseback and in 1932 famously resisted the Australian Army in what became known as the Great Emu War.

Australia is also home to most of the world's most venomous snakes, spiders and marine creatures. The continent did not evolve to make visitors comfortable. It evolved to survive. The same isolation that produced the platypus also produced the taipan, the funnel-web spider and the box jellyfish. Living here requires attention to what lives alongside. Australians learn this early.

At dusk in the Australian bush, kangaroos emerge from the scrub to graze. Rainbow lorikeets roost noisily in the eucalyptus. A kookaburra laughs from somewhere in the canopy. The platypus surfaces briefly in the river, then is gone. This is not a nature documentary. This is evening here.

16 The Rock at the Centre of Everything

School holidays. The family has flown to the Northern Territory. It is their first time. They are standing at the base of Uluru at sunrise. The rock glows red-orange in the morning light. Everyone is quiet.

Navya: *(whispering)* Why are we whispering?

Dad: *(quietly)* Because it feels like that kind of place.

Arjun: How old is it?

Dad: The rock itself formed about 550 million years ago. But the Anangu people have been living here and caring for this Country for at least 30,000 years.

Arjun: And they do not want people to climb it?

Dad: They asked people not to for decades. In 2019 climbing was permanently closed. Uluru is a sacred site. To the Anangu it is not a tourist attraction. It is a living part of their law and their Dreaming.

Navya: So all those years people just climbed it anyway?

Dad: Many did. Some understood. Some did not.

The light shifts. The rock changes colour from orange to deep red.

Navya: It is like it is breathing.

Dad: That is the light. But I know what you mean.

Stand far enough back from Uluru and it takes your breath away. Not because it is tall. At 348 metres it is smaller than many mountains. But because it has no obvious reason to be here. In the middle of one of the flattest, driest landscapes on Earth, a single sandstone formation rises from the plain like something placed from another world. The Anangu people are the traditional custodians of Uluru, which they have known as a living, sacred site for at least 30,000 years. To them it is not a geological curiosity. It is the physical trace of ancestral beings from the Dreaming, a place where law, knowledge and responsibility meet. Every crack, waterhole and cave in the rock carries meaning that can take a lifetime to understand.

For much of the twentieth century Uluru was known as Ayers Rock, a name given by European surveyors in 1873. The site was returned to the Anangu in 1985 in one of the most significant land rights decisions in Australian history. The joint management arrangement that followed became an early model for how traditional custodianship and conservation could operate together.

The most contested issue was climbing. Tourists had been walking to the summit since the 1950s. The Anangu asked visitors not to climb from the beginning, explaining that the route crossed a path of deep spiritual significance. Signs at the base carried this request. Guides repeated it. For decades many tourists still climbed, some out of ignorance, others out of indifference. The mountain was there and it could be climbed, and for a long time that was reason enough. In October 2019, after decades of advocacy and a broader shift in attitudes toward First Nations authority, climbing was permanently closed.

The outback that surrounds Uluru is itself one of the most extreme environments on Earth. More than 70 percent of the Australian continent is arid or semi arid. In the red centre the silence feels physical, as if sound itself has been stretched thin. The horizon runs so flat and so far that the sky feels larger than anywhere else. Light changes the landscape constantly, from soft pink at dawn to deep red at midday to violet at dusk. It is an ancient environment in a geological sense, shaped over immense time spans, though not in the literal sense of being older than life on Earth. Most Australians never travel here, yet many feel it belongs to them in some quiet, inherited way. The outback is not just a place. It is part of how the country understands itself.

Voices From Country: "Uluru is a very sacred place. It is quiet and peaceful, and we want it to stay that way." This is how Anangu traditional owners have described their relationship with Uluru to visitors for decades. The Anangu do not object to people visiting. They ask that people visit as guests on someone else's Country, with the same respect they would bring to a cathedral or a temple. Tjukurpa, the Anangu law that governs the site, has been maintained and passed down for thousands of generations. It does not need to be explained. It needs to be respected.

17 The Ground Beneath Your Feet

A Saturday morning at home. Dad is listening to the financial news on the kitchen radio. Iron ore prices have dropped. Arjun comes in.

Arjun: Why does the Australian economy care so much about iron ore prices? We do not make steel here.

Dad: We dig it up and sell it to China who makes the steel. We have the rocks. They have the factories.

Arjun: Is that a problem?

Dad: When the price is high, the economy does well. When it falls we are in trouble. The wealth is not evenly spread either. Some parts of the country have been completely transformed by mining. Others have seen almost nothing.

Navya: *(appearing in her pyjamas)* What is in the ground?

Dad: Iron, coal, gold, lithium, uranium.

Navya: Are they running out?

Dad: Not yet. That is the other part of the argument.

Australia is one of the most resource rich countries on Earth. The ground beneath it holds vast quantities of iron ore, coal, gold, natural gas, lithium and uranium. These are not marginal deposits. They are among the largest known reserves globally. For most of Australia's modern history, extracting and exporting these resources has been a central engine of the economy.

The quarry economy, a phrase used both admiringly and critically, describes a model in which Australia's main role in the global system is the extraction and export of raw materials. The resources are shipped overseas for processing and manufacturing, then returned as finished goods or value in financial form. When global prices are high the economy expands. When they fall Australia feels the impact. Over time this model has left relatively limited domestic manufacturing capacity compared to the scale of extraction.

The debate has become sharper with climate change. Australia's coal exports sit in tension with global efforts to reduce emissions. Yet the quarry economy now faces a shift rather than an ending. Australia holds significant deposits of lithium, a key mineral in electric vehicle batteries and energy storage systems. The same geology that powered the fossil fuel era may also support parts of the energy transition.

The benefits of mining are also unevenly distributed. Some regions have been transformed almost overnight, with new infrastructure, jobs and investment. Other areas, particularly remote and rural communities away from extraction hubs, see less direct benefit and more indirect disruption. The quarry economy has made Australia wealthy in aggregate, but that average masks persistent regional and social differences that remain a continuing source of debate.

The phrase "dig it up and ship it out" captures part of Australia's historical economic story. Whether it defines its future is less certain. The ground beneath the country still matters deeply, but what it yields, and how much of it stays, is now part of a broader question about where Australia is heading next.

Did You Know? The Pilbara region of Western Australia contains the world's largest known deposits of iron ore. Australia sells approximately 900 million tonnes of iron ore per year, the vast majority to China. This single trade relationship between a remote corner of Western Australia and Chinese steel mills is one of the most consequential economic connections in the world. It makes Australia's economy uniquely vulnerable to decisions made in Beijing and uniquely dependent on a relationship that is also its greatest strategic anxiety.

Story - Alec Fong Lim at First Light

Darwin, Northern Territory · December 25, 1974

Alec Fong Lim steps out of what remains of his office and looks at his city.

There is no city. There is debris from one end of the horizon to the other. Cyclone Tracy came in the early hours of Christmas morning with winds that the instruments could not measure because the instruments were destroyed. The storm is gone now. The sky is clear. The air is absolutely still in the way that air is still only after enormous violence.

He is the Lord Mayor of Darwin. His family has been in the Top End for three generations, Chinese Australians who came to Darwin when it was a frontier town and stayed when it became a city. This is his city. He knows every street, every building, every neighbourhood. He is walking through it now and he cannot find it.

Sixty-five people are dead. Forty-nine thousand people are homeless. Every structure in the city is damaged. Most are gone. He has been awake since the storm hit. He has been moving through the wreckage since the wind dropped. There are decisions to make that no manual covers. Water. Medical supplies. Communication with the mainland. Evacuation. Darwin has to be emptied before disease and heat do what the cyclone started.

He stops at a corner he recognises, though the buildings around it are gone. He stood here as a boy with his grandfather, who stood here with his father. Three generations of Fong Lims on this corner, watching Darwin become something. His grandfather came when the White Australia Policy was still in force, navigating a country that officially did not want him here. He stayed. He built. He raised children who built. Now Alec Fong Lim stands in the rubble of what they built and begins the work of deciding how to build it again.

He takes out his notebook and starts a list.

Darwin was rebuilt. It is today a thriving city of 150,000 people, the most Asian-facing capital in Australia. Alec Fong Lim served as Lord Mayor until 1975 and is remembered as the man who held Darwin together in the hours after Tracy.

Darwin today is one of the most ethnically diverse capital cities in Australia. The man who rebuilt it after the worst natural disaster in the country's history was the grandson of a Chinese immigrant who came when Australia officially did not want him here.

18 The Cities That Surprise the World

The family is at a café in Melbourne on a Saturday morning. Oliver and Mei are there too. The café says their coffee is best in the area. Outside, the laneway is full of street art.

Oliver: My cousins from London visited last month. They said Melbourne was nothing like what they expected.

Arjun: What did they expect?

Oliver: Kangaroos, I think. The outback. Not this.

Mei: My grandparents said the same thing when they arrived. They thought Australia was a country town. Then they saw the harbour in Sydney.

Dad: Australia has some of the most liveable cities on Earth. Melbourne has been ranked the world's most liveable city multiple times. And most people outside Australia have no idea.

Navya: Because of the coffee?

Dad: Partly because of the coffee.

Arjun: Why is Melbourne coffee so famous anyway?

Dad: Italian migrants in the 1950s. They brought their coffee culture and it took over. Melbourne has a genuine café culture that rivals anything in Europe.

Navya: *(taking a sip)* That tracks.

Most people who visit Australia for the first time say the same thing. They expected the outback. They did not expect this. The cities that line Australia's coastline are among the most liveable, most beautiful and most surprising on Earth. They are also where almost everyone actually lives.

Sydney is perhaps the most beautiful harbour city in the world. The Opera House, completed in 1973 after fourteen years of construction and enormous controversy, is now one of the most recognised buildings on Earth. The Danish architect Jørn Utzon won the design competition in 1957 with a concept that engineers said was impossible to build. It was eventually built anyway, and it transformed what a public building could be. The Harbour Bridge, completed in 1932, is equally iconic. Together they define a skyline that announces itself as extraordinary.

Melbourne operates differently. Where Sydney dazzles with its harbour, Melbourne charms with its laneways. The inner city is threaded with narrow alleys full of cafés, street art, bookshops and restaurants representing every cuisine on Earth. Melbourne has been ranked the world's most liveable city more times than any other, a title based on stability, healthcare, culture, environment and education. It takes the ranking seriously. It also takes its coffee seriously, having built a genuine café culture from the espresso traditions brought by Italian and Greek migrants in the 1950s that has since influenced coffee culture around the world.

The rivalry between Sydney and Melbourne is one of Australia's great ongoing arguments. Sydney people say Melbourne is cold and obsessed with coffee. Melbourne people say Sydney is shallow and obsessed with its harbour. Both are partly right. The rivalry has produced better cities. Each watches the other and raises its game.

Beyond the two great capitals, Australia's cities are genuinely diverse in character. Brisbane is subtropical, outdoors-oriented, growing fast and increasingly confident. Perth is the world's most isolated major city, closer to Singapore than to Sydney, shaped by the mining boom and by a relationship with Asia that is more immediate than anywhere else in the country. Adelaide is compact, gracious and underrated, with some of the best food and wine in Australia and a self-deprecating awareness that it is overlooked. Darwin, in the tropical north, is the most Asian-facing city in the country, a frontier town that has been rebuilt twice and carries its history lightly.

What Australian cities share is a quality of life that regularly surprises visitors. Beaches accessible from the city centre. Restaurants representing every cuisine on Earth. Public spaces that are genuinely used. A casualness in social interaction that reflects the national character. The people who live in these cities are not pretending to live somewhere else. The cities are where Australians actually are. And they are very good at it.

19 The Defeat That Became a Sacred Story

April 25th. The family is at the Shrine of Remembrance for the Dawn Service. Cold and dark. Thousands standing quietly. The Last Post plays.

Afterwards, walking back to the car in the grey morning light.

Arjun: Why does this feel more like a religion than a public holiday?

Dad: Because for a lot of Australians it is.

Arjun: We lost at Gallipoli. Why do we commemorate a failure?

Dad: Because for many Australians it was never really about winning or losing.

Arjun: What was it about then?

Dad: How the soldiers behaved. The courage. The care for one another. The story became more important than the outcome.

Arjun: Were there soldiers from all over Australia?

Dad: From everywhere. Farmers, factory workers, men who had never left their home state. They came from all over the continent and found themselves on a peninsula in Turkey.

Navya takes Dad's hand.

Navya: The Last Post is the saddest song in the world.

Anzac Day, April 25th, the anniversary of the landing at Gallipoli in 1915, is the most sacred day on the Australian calendar. More Australians attend Anzac Dawn Services than attend any church service at Christmas or Easter. The Gallipoli campaign was a military disaster. The Allied plan to force through the Dardanelles and capture Constantinople was conceived as a quick operation, expected to last weeks. It lasted eight months. The Australian and New Zealand Army Corps were pinned on narrow beaches under the heights of the peninsula and could not advance. When they were finally evacuated, Australian casualties were approximately 8,000 dead and 18,000 wounded.

Despite the failure Gallipoli became the founding myth of the Australian nation. The stories that came back were stories of courage under fire, soldiers going back for their mates and a refusal to be broken by impossible conditions. The Anzac spirit, as it became known, stood for endurance, fierce loyalty and an irreverence toward rank and authority that felt distinctly Australian. Something real was forged on those beaches. Something the country needed to believe about itself.

The Anzac story has grown over time. For most of the twentieth century it focused almost entirely on the men who fought. Gradually it has expanded to include the women who served, the Aboriginal soldiers, the non-British migrants who enlisted alongside them. The story is being told more fully now than it ever was. That is not a weakening of it. That is the country learning to see itself more honestly.

The relationship between Anzac Day and national identity has shifted across generations. For those who fought it was personal. For later generations it became symbolic. One small tradition captures the spirit perfectly. Anzac biscuits, made from oats and golden syrup, were sent by Australian women to soldiers overseas because they kept well on long sea voyages. They are still baked and eaten every April 25th. A biscuit that could survive the journey home became the taste of remembrance.

The Shrine forecourt at dawn is not a comfortable place. It is an honest one.

True Story: The Road They Built for Their Mates - The Great Ocean Road stretches 243 kilometres along the Victorian coastline. It is one of the most beautiful drives in the world. Most people who drive it do not know what it is. After the First World War, returned soldiers built it by hand with picks and shovels through rugged coastal terrain. It took fourteen years. The soldiers insisted on doing it themselves rather than using machinery. They wanted to build it with their hands as a tribute to the 60,000 Australians who did not come home. It is the largest war memorial in the world. It is also a road. Both things at once, which is very Australian.

20 The Insult That Became a Compliment

A rainy autumn afternoon. Dad has pulled Donald Horne's "The Lucky Country" from the shelf. Arjun has been flicking through it.

Arjun: This book is called "The Lucky Country" but the author seems angry throughout.

Dad: He was. It was not a compliment. He meant Australia had been succeeding by accident, not by excellence.

Arjun: And Australians heard it as a compliment?

Dad: Completely. Horne spent the rest of his life horrified that his warning had become a slogan.

Arjun: Is that ironic or just funny?

Dad: Both. And it says something true about Australia. A country comfortable with luck. That does not feel the need to prove itself.

Navya looks up from her drawing.

Navya: Are we lucky?

Dad: Very.

Navya: Then why is it raining?

Dad: Even lucky countries get rain, Navya.

Donald Horne was a journalist, academic and social critic who spent much of his career trying to shake Australia out of what he saw as comfortable mediocrity. In 1964 he published a book called *The Lucky Country*. Its opening sentence has become one of the most quoted sentences in Australian literature. "Australia is a lucky country, run mainly by second-rate people who share its luck." Horne's argument was a critique. Australia's prosperity derived from abundant natural resources, geographic insulation and good fortune. It had not earned its wealth through ingenuity or institutional excellence. It had been handed it by geography and history.

Australians read this as a compliment. The phrase entered the national vocabulary as an expression of pride and gratitude. It appeared in tourism campaigns, real estate advertisements and political speeches. A car manufacturer used it in television commercials. Horne watched this misreading spread with frustration until his death in 2005 but he could not dislodge it. The misreading had become the meaning.

There is something revealing in this. A country that is genuinely comfortable with luck has a particular kind of confidence, not the confidence of achievement but the confidence of sufficiency. Things are good enough. The sun is warm. The beaches are there. Why strain? Critics argue that this complacency has prevented Australia from building the industries and institutions it needs for the century ahead. That the coal and iron ore will not last forever. That the luck may run out.

The lucky country idea has also shaped how Australia responds to crisis. When things go wrong the instinct is often to wait for the luck to return rather than to fundamentally change the system that failed. The mining boom will come back. The drought will break. This optimism is sometimes warranted and sometimes catastrophically wrong.

But there is something to be said for a country that does not take itself too seriously. That wears its luck with a grin rather than a ceremony. Australia has produced world-class scientists, artists, architects, athletes and thinkers. It has built institutions that other countries have copied. It has taken in migrants from every corner of the world and made them Australian within a generation. The luck was real. But so was the work. Horne saw the complacency. He may have underestimated the quiet competence that ran alongside it.

Strange But True: Donald Horne lived to see "the lucky country" become one of the most celebrated phrases in Australian life, used proudly by politicians and advertisers and tourism campaigns. In later interviews he described the misreading as "a sad irony" and "a typical Australian failure to understand criticism." He had written a warning. Australia had turned it into a brand. He died in 2005 having never stopped trying to explain what he had actually meant.

21 The Bush That Never Leaves You

School holidays. The family stops at a Grampians lookout in the late afternoon. Red rock, blue-green eucalyptus, enormous sky. They get out and stand in the quiet.

Arjun: Why is this more "Australian" in our minds than the city?

Dad: We live in Melbourne. Five million people. But when someone says Australia, people imagine this.

Arjun: Why though? Nobody actually lives out here.

Dad: That is exactly the question. That is the bush myth. The idea that the real Australia lives out here even though almost nobody does.

Arjun: But why did an urban country build a rural mythology?

Dad: Because the city felt like Britain. The bush was the thing that was actually Australian, alien and vast and like nowhere else on Earth.

Navya climbs onto a rock.

Navya: I love it here. But I would not want to live here.

Dad: Most Australians agree with you.

Navya: Where are the kangaroos?

Dad: Right out there somewhere.

More than 85 percent of Australians live in cities, concentrated in the coastal capitals. Sydney, Melbourne, Brisbane, Perth, Adelaide, dense, cosmopolitan, connected to the world. Australia is one of the most urbanised countries on Earth. And yet its national identity is built almost entirely around the bush, the outback and the red centre, the places where almost no one lives.

The bush myth holds that the real Australia is rural and that the national character was forged in the struggles of the outback rather than the offices of the city. The swagman. The drover. The stockman riding alone across a vast red plain. These are the images Australia reaches for when it wants to describe itself.

The myth was constructed largely in the 1890s through the work of poets and writers including Henry Lawson and Banjo Paterson and Dorothea Mackellar. They asked what made Australia different from Britain and found the answer in the landscape, harsh and alien and like nowhere else on Earth. The paradox is that most of these artists lived in Sydney and Melbourne. The bush they celebrated was not where they spent their time. It was an idea of Australia rather than a description of where Australians actually lived.

That gap between where Australians live and what they imagine as their heartland has never closed. Australians are the most likely people in the world to live in a large city and yet feel their soul belongs somewhere in the red dust interior. They drive out to the bush for long weekends. They hang paintings of the outback in their city apartments. They feel a pull toward a landscape most of them visit only occasionally and know mostly through art and story.

The bush myth has given the country something genuine. A sense of the land as something vast and ancient and beyond human control. A humility before the landscape that is not common in more densely populated countries. The longing for the red centre that most Australians carry without ever going there is one of the most distinctly Australian things there is.

Strange But True: "My Country," the poem by Dorothea Mackellar containing the famous lines about "a sunburnt country, a land of sweeping plains, of ragged mountain ranges, of droughts and flooding rains," one of the most quoted poems in Australian history, was written in England by a young woman who was homesick for Australia. The defining celebration of the Australian landscape was composed somewhere else entirely. Perhaps the bush myth has always been partly about longing for something you are not quite in.

22 The Accent That Tells You Where You Belong

A Sunday afternoon in the backyard. The family is having lunch outside. Mei is over. The radio is on in the background.

Mei: I love how we Australians shorten everything. This afternoon becomes "arvo." Service station becomes "servo." McDonald's becomes "Macca's."

Arjun: Sunglasses are "sunnies." Breakfast is "brekkie." Brisbane is "Brizzy."

Dad: It is one of the most distinctive things about Australian English. If a word can be shortened and a vowel swapped at the end, Australians will do it.

Mei: Why?

Dad: Nobody knows for certain. Some think it came from the convict era, where informal speech was a small act of defiance. Some think it just evolved because Australians like to feel relaxed about everything, including words.

Navya considers this.

Navya: In India Grandma calls me "Navya." Here my friends call me "Nav."

Dad: And both are you.

Navya: That is very Australian.

Australian English is one of the most instantly recognisable varieties of English in the world. The accent emerged from a remarkable convergence. Tens of thousands of people from different parts of Britain and Ireland arrived in the colony within a few generations and a new accent formed that belonged to none of them and to all of them. It was not a British accent. It was not like any accent anywhere else. It was something entirely new, shaped by the mix of voices and the conditions of the country.

The vocabulary is equally distinctive. The habit of shortening words and adding a diminutive sound at the end, an o or a y or an ie, is almost uniquely Australian. Arvo, servo, rego, sunnies, brekkie, choccy, footy, barbie. The words signal membership. A person who uses them naturally is understood to be Australian or to have become Australian. They also carry a particular attitude. A preference for the casual over the formal, the warm over the impressive. Australian English resists pretension. It shrinks long words down to size and turns strangers into mates.

Australian English also carries the history of migration. Words from Aboriginal languages have entered everyday speech including kangaroo, wallaby, wombat, budgerigar, boomerang and hundreds of place names. Words from Greek, Italian, Lebanese and Vietnamese communities have filled the food vocabulary and the daily language of Australian cities. Each wave of migration has left its mark on the way the country speaks.

The accent itself has shifted over the decades. Linguists identify three broad varieties from broad to cultivated with general Australian in the middle. The broad accent thickens the vowels and flattens the intonation. Most Australians sit somewhere between. The way a person speaks still carries information about where they grew up and sometimes which suburb their parents came from.

Some of the words that came into Australian English from Aboriginal languages are now known worldwide. But thousands of other words from hundreds of languages have been lost. Communities across Australia are working to bring those languages back, teaching them to children, recording elders, returning words to the places that carry them. The young oldest country is trying to remember what it almost forgot.

Worth Knowing: More than 250 Aboriginal languages were spoken before European settlement. Approximately 120 are still spoken today, though many by only a handful of elderly speakers. About 20 are still being learned by children as a first language. The loss of a language is the loss of an entire way of understanding the world. Some communities have successfully brought languages back from the edge of extinction. The young oldest country is trying to remember what it almost forgot.

23 The Sport That Stops a Nation

December. Dad, Arjun and Oliver are at the MCG for the Boxing Day Test. Hot and packed. At lunch break, eating in their seats.

Oliver: Why is cricket such a big deal here? It takes five days and still might not have a result.

Dad: Because for over a hundred years, beating England at cricket was the closest thing Australia had to declaring independence.

Oliver: Really?

Dad: Every time Australia beat England it was proof the colony had surpassed the mother country.

Arjun: Is that still what it means?

Dad: Less so. But sport in Australia still carries identity in a way that goes beyond recreation. Which sport you follow says something about where you are from. AFL is Victoria, South Australia and Western Australia. Rugby league is New South Wales and Queensland.

Oliver: My family follows soccer. Because of my grandparents.

Dad: Exactly. The map of Australian sport is the map of Australian immigration. Your grandparents brought their game with them.

Australia takes a wicket. Oliver and Arjun both jump up cheering.

Oliver: *(sitting back down, grinning)* Okay. I think I understand cricket now.

Dad: No one ever fully understands cricket. That is also part of it.

Few countries of Australia's size produce world-class athletes across as many disciplines. A nation of 28 million has consistently competed at the highest levels in swimming, cricket, AFL, rugby, tennis, cycling, rowing and athletics. The depth of that achievement is remarkable. The cultural investment begins young and runs deep. Saturday morning sport is a national institution. Parents at every school, every oval, every pool compare notes on which competition their child is playing in, which team, which coach. The pathway from Saturday morning to representing Australia feels real because it often is. In Australia, sport is not just recreation. It is a primary language of identity.

That language varies by geography. AFL, which originated in Melbourne in 1858, dominates Victoria, South Australia and Western Australia. Rugby league, with its heartland in western Sydney and south-east Queensland, rules New South Wales and Queensland. The rivalry runs deep and loud. Mention football in a room of Australians and someone will immediately ask which sport you mean. You can almost tell where someone grew up by what they call football.

AFL itself is one of the world's most distinctly local sports. It developed on the playing fields of Melbourne in the 1850s partly to keep cricketers fit in winter and evolved into a high-speed aerial game unlike anything played anywhere else. The rules, the oval ground, the scoring system. None of it resembles any other football code. It is Australian in the most literal sense. Invented here. Played almost nowhere else. Loved with an intensity that outsiders find difficult to understand.

Cricket occupies a special place above all codes. For much of Australia's colonial history, beating England at cricket was the most satisfying proof that the colony had grown up. The Ashes, the test series between Australia and England played since 1882, was for generations the most important sporting contest in Australian life. That feeling has faded as Australia has grown more confident of its own identity. But the Boxing Day Test at the MCG still draws eighty thousand people on a hot December day. Australia has won more Cricket World Cups than any other nation, a record that reflects a country that does not just love the game but has made it its own.

Soccer, for a long time dismissed by some Australians as "wog ball," has grown into one of the most popular sports. The map of Australian sport is the map of Australian immigration. Each wave of migrants brought their game and slowly it became part of the landscape.

Worth Knowing: Australia has hosted the Olympic Games twice and will host again. Melbourne in 1956 was the first Olympics held in the Southern Hemisphere. Sydney in 2000 was rated by many athletes as the greatest Games ever staged, with Australia finishing fourth on the medal table. Brisbane will host the 2032 Games, making Australia only the second country after the United States to host the Summer Olympics three times.

Australia has also produced swimmers of extraordinary dominance. Dawn Fraser won gold in the 100 metres freestyle at three consecutive Olympics. Ariarne Titmus won gold in the 400 metres and 800 metres freestyle at Paris in 2024, the latest in a long line of Australian swimmers who have redefined what is possible in the pool.

But the moment that stopped the country came on a running track. At the 2000 Sydney Olympics, Cathy Freeman lit the Olympic cauldron at the opening ceremony and then, eight days later, won the 400 metres final wrapped in both the Australian and Aboriginal flags. When she crossed the finish line the stadium of 112,000 people produced a sound witnesses say they had never heard before. It was not just a sporting moment. It was a statement about who Australia was and who it was trying to become.

The Formula One Grand Prix in Melbourne each March is a different kind of moment. The opening race of the season draws the entire world's attention to Albert Park for a weekend. The streets around the lake fill with hundreds of thousands of people. The city stops. For four days Melbourne is not a distant city at the edge of the world. It is the centre of it.

Beyond the track and the pool, Australia has produced tennis champions of extraordinary consistency. Rod Laver, Margaret Court, Lleyton Hewitt, Ash Barty. Rugby world champions. The range is the point. This is not a country that is good at one thing.

When players from migrant backgrounds represent Australia, when communities that once felt like outsiders see themselves in the national jersey, something shifts. That diversity is not just a pleasant fact. It is a competitive advantage. Australia draws athletes from every culture that has made its home here. The sporting field was where Australia first worked out in public what it meant to be a new kind of country. It is still doing that work today.

Worth Knowing: The Melbourne Cup, held on the first Tuesday in November, is the only sporting event in the world that is a public holiday in the city where it is held. Offices stop. People who have never bet on anything else put five dollars on a horse. The Cup is an annual collective pause in which Australia briefly agrees to do the same thing at the same time regardless of background or state. That consensus is rare enough in this country to be worth noting.

Story - Ash Barty at Melbourne Park

Melbourne Park · January 29, 2022

Ash Barty bounces the ball and does not think about the crowd.

She is twenty-five years old and she has been here before, at the baseline of a Grand Slam final, knowing exactly what she needs to do. She has been world number one for over two years. She has won Wimbledon and the French Open. But this is Melbourne. This is her country. This is the one that has waited forty-four years for an Australian woman to win it. The last Australian woman to win the Australian Open before her was Chris O'Neil in 1978.

The crowd at Rod Laver Arena is nearly 15,000 people and they are all breathing together.

She bounces the ball again. She thinks about the process. Not the scoreboard, not the history, not the forty-four years. The process. The next point. The ball in her hand. She learned this the hard way. At eighteen she walked away from tennis altogether. She said she was not happy and she left. She played cricket. She worked. She found herself. And then she came back.

Coming back was her choice. Winning on her terms was her choice. Everything from here has been her choice.

She serves.

In under two hours, it is over. She has won 6-3, 7-6. She falls to her knees on the blue hardcourt. Her coach runs to her. Her team runs to her. The crowd makes a sound that feels like it fills the whole city.

She is of Ngarigo heritage. She grew up in Ipswich, Queensland. She plays for herself and for Australia and she carries both without contradiction. She has always known who she is.

Three months later, still ranked world number one, she retires. On her own terms. Because she is ready.

Ash Barty remains the most recent Australian woman to win the Australian Open. She stepped away from the game at the very top and left it exactly as she chose to. She did it her way.

24 The Country That Said Stay Different

A Saturday in late November. The family is at the Queen Victoria Market for the weekly shop. They are moving through the fruit and vegetable hall. Mum has a basket. Navya is eating a jam doughnut.

Navya: *(stopping)* Look. That stall has dragon fruit. That one has bitter melon. That one has curry leaves. And that one has fresh figs.

Arjun: The whole hall smells incredible.

Dad: This market has been here since 1878. It has always looked like whoever just arrived in Melbourne.

Arjun: So the market is basically a map of immigration?

Dad: Exactly. The gold rush brought the first wave. Then postwar migrants from Greece, Italy and Malta. Then families from Vietnam, Lebanon and China. Each wave brought their food and their recipes and their way of doing things.

Mum: And eventually their stall at the Queen Vic.

Dad: In the 1970s Australia made a deliberate choice. Instead of asking newcomers to disappear into Australian culture, it asked them to stay different. To keep their language and their food and their festivals.

Arjun: Did that work?

Navya: *(already at the next stall, pointing)* I want one of everything.

Dad: That is the answer.

After decades of telling migrants to become Australian by abandoning who they were, Australia made a different choice.

From the 1970s onward, the policy became explicitly multicultural. The idea was that migrants could keep their language, their food, their festivals and their culture while still being fully Australian. Australia was not one thing you had to become. It was many things you could be at once.

This was controversial. Many Australians worried it would tear the country apart. What happened instead was that it made the country more interesting, more resourceful and more connected to the world.

Today approximately 30 percent of Australians were born overseas. More than 300 languages are spoken in Australian homes. Sydney has one of the largest Chinese communities outside China. Melbourne has the largest Greek population outside Greece. The food, the music, the architecture and the culture of every Australian city has been shaped by wave after wave of new arrivals.

Every one of them added something. The Australia of today is not the Australia of 1788 or 1901 or even 1970. It is the accumulated result of every arrival, every contribution, every person who came and stayed and built something.

That is not a complication of the Australian story. It is the Australian story.

The multicultural model has not been without tensions. Questions about immigration levels and cultural change have been live debates in every election cycle. But the foundational bet Australia made in the 1970s, that diversity is a strength rather than a threat, has not been reversed by any government of any political persuasion. Most Australians, looking at what their cities have become, can see that it worked.

Worth Knowing: SBS, the Special Broadcasting Service, was established in 1977 specifically to serve Australia's multicultural communities. It broadcasts in over 60 languages and produces news, documentaries and drama in languages from Arabic to Mandarin to Greek to Hindi. The fact that Australia created a national broadcaster specifically to speak to its migrants in their own languages says something important about what kind of multiculturalism Australia chose. Not assimilation. Representation.

25 The Argument That Became the Identity

Christmas Eve. The family is on Bourke Street in the city to see the Myer Christmas windows. They have been in the queue for forty-five minutes and are almost at the front. Navya is stretching to see the first window. Arjun, Dad and Mum are behind her.

Arjun: Dad, is the new social media ban a "fair go"? It feels like another one of those fences we saw in the new suburbs.

Dad: Some see it as a fence, Arjun. Others see it as a safety rail, keeping you off the digital road until you're ready to drive. It's our newest national argument.

Arjun: That's the thing. Do you think Australia ever knows what it is? Other countries seem more settled. They know their story. We just keep arguing. About fences, flags, everything.

Dad: Does that bother you?

Arjun: No. I think it might be the best thing about it.

Navya: (*pushes forward with eyes wide open*) I know what Australia is.

Arjun: What?

Navya: This. All these different people standing together looking at the same window.

Long pause.

Dad: That might be the most accurate answer of all.

Every country has a story it tells about itself. Some stories are settled, agreed upon and taught without question. Australia's story is not like that. It is argued about, revised and slowly expanded to include voices that were left out for too long. That is not a weakness. It is a sign that the country is still paying attention.

The argument is uncomfortable sometimes. But a country that keeps questioning its own story is a country that has not given up on getting it right. The argument keeps the question alive. And a question kept alive can, eventually, be answered.

The 25 ideas in this book are a frame, a way of seeing the young oldest country through its ideas rather than its dates. Its concepts rather than its events. The land is ancient. The cultures that read it are ancient. The nation built on it is very young. And what that nation will become is genuinely undecided. That undecidedness is not a failure. It is an invitation.

What makes Australia's argument different from most is that it is conducted in good faith. Australians disagree loudly and often, about history, about who belongs, about what the country owes and what it has earned. But the argument happens inside a democracy that has held for over a century. It happens in a society that has repeatedly chosen to extend rather than restrict its sense of who counts. That is not nothing. That is actually quite rare.

The arguments that matter most are the ones that have no easy answer. Whether Australia should become a republic. How to properly recognise the First Nations peoples who were here before the country existed. How to balance the demands of economic growth with the health of the continent's ancient ecosystems. How to be both a Pacific nation and a country with deep ties to Europe and America. None of these arguments will be settled in a single election or a single generation. That is what makes them worth having.

Worth Knowing: In 2023 Australia held a referendum on whether to establish a First Nations Voice to Parliament, an advisory body that would give Aboriginal and Torres Strait Islander peoples a formal say on laws and policies affecting them. The proposal was defeated, with 60 percent voting no. It was a significant moment not because of the result but because the question had been asked at all. The debate that surrounded it was one of the most serious national conversations about identity and belonging that Australia had ever had in public.

Australia is also one of the few countries in the world where the national argument is genuinely open. Where the founding story is contested not just by academics but by ordinary people at kitchen tables and in parliament and in the street. Where what it means to be Australian is still up for discussion rather than fixed by tradition or force.

That openness has a cost. It can feel unsettling to live in a country that has not made up its mind about itself. Other countries have certainties about their heroes, their history, their place in the world. Australia holds its certainties more lightly. The heroes get questioned. The history gets revised. The place in the world keeps shifting.

But that openness is also a gift. A country that can still argue about its founding story is a country that has not yet closed off the possibility of getting it right. The Uluru Statement, the reconciliation movement, the republic debate, the changing face of the national teams. All of these are expressions of a country that believes it can still become something better than it has been.

The ancient songlines are still being sung. The gold rush cities are still growing. The reef is still being argued over. The teams still look more like the country every year. The conversation at the kitchen table has not ended. It never will.

What the young oldest country keeps discovering is that the argument itself is part of the identity. Australia does not know exactly what it is. It knows it is worth arguing about. And a country that believes it is worth arguing about has already answered the most important question of all.

True Story: The Apology - On February 13, 2008, Prime Minister Kevin Rudd stood in parliament and said one word no Australian government had ever said before. Sorry. He was apologising to the Stolen Generations, the Aboriginal and Torres Strait Islander children removed from their families by government policy between 1910 and 1970. Tens of thousands of Aboriginal Australians watched in public spaces across the country. Many had waited their whole lives for that moment. Many did not live to see it. It did not undo what was done. But it was the first time Australia's government looked directly at part of its history and said, without qualification, that it was wrong.

Conclusion

Late Christmas night. The family is driving home from the city. They went back in after lunch to see the lights. Navya is already asleep in the back, still wearing the tinsel she found at the market. Arjun is looking out the window at the quiet streets.

Arjun: *(quietly)* Of all the ideas we talked about this year, which one do you think is the most important?

Dad parks in the driveway and turns off the engine. He does not answer straight away.

Dad: The one we have not finished with yet.

Arjun: Which one is that?

Dad: All of them.

Arjun thinks about this.

Arjun: That is not an answer.

Dad: It is the truest one I have.

In the back seat Navya stirs.

Navya: *(barely awake)* Are we home?

Dad: Yes.

She goes back to sleep. They sit in the driveway for a moment. The street is quiet. The summer night is warm and full of crickets. The young oldest country, still becoming itself, all around them.

Australia is a country built on ancient foundations, disturbed by colonisation, shaped by conflict and compromise, remade by migration and still arguing about what it is. That argument is not a weakness. It is the most honest thing about the place.

The 65,000 years before 1788 are not prologue. They are history. The two hundred and fifty years since are not the whole story. They are a chapter.

The 25 ideas in this book are not a complete picture. They are a way in. A country this complex and this old and this young cannot be understood in a single book or a single conversation or a single year of backyard discussions. What it can be is approached. Wondered at. Argued about. That is what this family has been doing. It is what Australians have always been doing.

Some of what you have read is uncomfortable. The frontier conflict that was never called a war. One of the first laws the new parliament passed. The original Australians excluded from the census of their own country until 1967. These things happened. They matter. A country that looks away from its difficult history repeats it. A country that looks at it honestly has a chance to do better.

But this book is not just about what went wrong. It is about what went right too. The democracy that grew from a goldfield rebellion. The welfare state built before most countries had imagined one. The multicultural society that emerged from one of the most restrictive immigration policies in the world. The conservation fights won. The languages being brought back from the edge of extinction. The athletes who ran their laps carrying both flags. These things happened too.

The young oldest country is not finished. It never will be. Every generation of Australians inherits this argument and adds to it. Yours will too. The questions this book asks, about land and fairness, about belonging and becoming, about what a country owes the people it was built on and the people it invited in, are not questions with final answers. They are questions worth spending a life with.

This book draws on a wide range of historical research, public records and cultural knowledge. Some of the ideas here are complex and still debated. And in places they have been simplified to make them easier to understand. Where there is disagreement, this book reflects widely accepted interpretations while recognising that Australia's story is not settled. It is not a final answer. It is part of the conversation.

That is what makes it worth telling.

Story - The Walk Across the Bridge

Sydney Harbour Bridge · May 28, 2000

Aunty Millie Ingram does not know how many people are behind her.

She is seventy-three years old and she has walked a long way in her life. This morning she walked from Circular Quay with her daughter and her grandchildren and joined the crowd that is now filling the Sydney Harbour Bridge from one end to the other. Nobody asked her to come. There was no government announcement, no official call. A few weeks ago someone said there would be a walk for reconciliation across the bridge and people began to make plans and the plans grew and grew until this.

The bridge holds perhaps a hundred thousand people at any one time. More are waiting at both ends. The total number who will walk today will reach three hundred thousand. It will be one of the largest public demonstrations in Australian history and nobody organised it. It simply happened because people decided to come.

Aunty Millie walks slowly. Her granddaughter holds her hand on one side. A young man she has never met holds her other arm, steadying her on the gradient. He is maybe twenty years old. He has a flag painted on his cheek. He has said nothing. He just appeared beside her when she slowed and has been there ever since.

Below them the harbour glitters. The Opera House stands white and impossible to the east. Sydney is enormous and blue and beautiful.

She thinks about what she wants her grandchildren to know. That this day happened. That three hundred thousand people chose to walk. That the country, when given the chance, sometimes chooses to be better than its history. The Aboriginal flag rests against her as she walks her lap. The country that made her runs that lap with her.

The Reconciliation Bridge Walk of 2000 remains the largest public act of support for reconciliation in Australian history. No politician called it. No government organised it. Three hundred thousand Australians simply decided to walk.

WALK FOR RECONCILIATION
UNITING OUR NATION
WALK FOR RECONCILIATION
UNITING OUR NATION

Rahul Agrawal is an Information Technology Consultant by profession and lives in Melbourne with his two children, Arjun and Navya. He came to Australia as an immigrant, drawn by the promise of a country that gave everyone a fair go regardless of where they started. He made Melbourne home and has been asking questions about it ever since. The conversations in this book began at his own kitchen table, when his children started asking the kind of questions that turned out not to have simple answers.

Arjun and Navya are the heart of this book. Arjun's curiosity and his habit of asking "but why?" are the engine behind every idea explored here. Navya's instinct to cut through to the simplest and most honest truth is the reason so many of the best lines in this book belong to a six-year-old. Their mother, who has listened to and shaped these conversations from the beginning, is the quiet reason they happen at all.

Rahul writes the One World Series with a belief that the best education asks questions before it provides answers, and that the most important questions are the ones a country is still asking about itself.

Australia gave this family a home. This book is their way of understanding it.

Also in the One World Series:

One Sky, Many Calendars : Why does the new year fall on different days around the world? Why do some cultures follow the moon and others the sun? From the Gregorian calendar to the Islamic Hijri, from the Jewish year to the ancient Vedic traditions, Book 1 of the One World Series explores the 25 ideas behind how human beings have measured time across every culture on Earth.

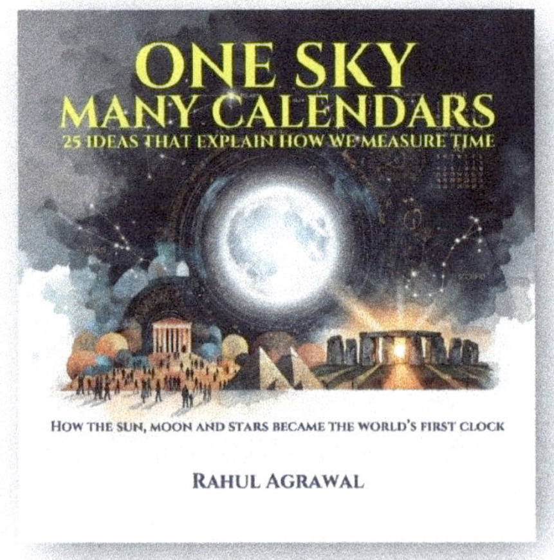

If you enjoyed this book please share it and consider leaving a review. These ideas are worth spreading.

www.ingramcontent.com/pod-product-compliance
Lightning Source LLC
Chambersburg PA
CBHW042049030726

47599CB00019B/2425